GOVERNING MOTIONS

Vote required?	Applies to what other motions?	Can have what other motions applied to it?	Refer to page
Majority	None	None	72
Majority	None	Amend†	70
None	None	None	66
Majority*	Main motion	None	62
2/3	Debatable motions	None	58
2/3	Debatable motions	Amend†	56
Majority	Main motion	Amend†, close debate, limit debate	53
Majority	Main motion	Amend†, close debate, limit debate	50
Majority	Rewordable motions	Close debate, limit debate	42
Majority	None	Specific main, subsidiary	30
Majority	Main motion	Close debate, limit debate	33
Majority	Main motion	Close debate, limit debate	37
Majority	Main motion	None	39

MOTIONS

Vote required?	Applies to what other motions?	Can have what other motions applied to it?	Refer to page
Majority	Decision of chair	Close debate, limit debate	77
2/3	None	None	79
Majority	Main motion	None	120
None	Any error	None	83
None	All motions	None	86
None	All motions	None	89
None	Main motion	None	91
None	Indecisive vote	None	94

Revision Committee
American Institute of Parliamentarians

Edwin C. Bliss, Chairman
Member, Advisory Council, AIP

Miriam Butcher
Former President, AIP

Joyce Parks
Member of the Board, AIP

Sanford Peterson
Member of the Board, AIP

Donald L. Wolfarth
Member of the Board, AIP

The Standard Code of Parliamentary Procedure

**THIRD EDITION
NEW AND REVISED**

by Alice Sturgis

McGRAW-HILL INC.

*New York   San Francisco   Washington, D.C.   Auckland   Bogotá
Caracas   Lisbon   London   Madrid   Mexico City   Milan
Montreal   New Delhi   San Juan   Singapore
Sydney   Tokyo   Toronto*

First McGraw-Hill paperback edition, 1993

3 4 5 6 7 8 9 0 F G R F G R 9 8 7 6 5 4

ISBN   0-07-062399-6   {HC}
ISBN   0-07-062522-0   {PBK}

Sturgis, Alice.
    The standard code of parliamentary procedure.

    "Revision Committee, American Institute of
Parliamentarians"—Half t.p.
    Includes index.
    1. Parliamentary practice.   I. American Institute
of Parliamentarians. Revision Committee.   II. Title.
JF515.S88   1988   060.4'2   65-24530
ISBN 0-07-062399-6 (hc)
ISBN 0-07-062522-0 (pbk)

CONTENTS

Chapter 4
CLASSIFICATION OF MOTIONS

Chapter 5
PRECEDENCE OF MOTIONS

Chapter 6
RULES GOVERNING MOTIONS

Chapter 7
MAIN MOTIONS

Chapter 8
SUBSIDIARY MOTIONS

MOTION TO AMEND

MOTION TO REFER TO COMMITTEE

MOTION TO POSTPONE DEFINITELY

Chapter 9
PRIVILEGED MOTIONS

Chapter 10
INCIDENTAL MOTIONS

Chapter 11
NOTICE OF MEETINGS AND PROPOSALS

Chapter 12
MEETINGS

Chapter 13
QUORUM

Chapter 14
ORDER OF BUSINESS

Chapter 15
DEBATE

Chapter 19
OFFICERS

Chapter 20
COMMITTEES AND BOARDS

Chapter 21
COMMITTEE REPORTS AND RECOMMENDATIONS

Chapter 22
CONVENTIONS AND THEIR COMMITTEES

Chapter 23
MINUTES

Chapter 24
CHARTERS, BYLAWS, AND RULES

Chapter 25
FINANCES

Chapter 26
LEGAL CLASSIFICATIONS OF ORGANIZATIONS

Chapter 27
RIGHTS OF MEMBERS AND OF ORGANIZATIONS

Chapter 28
STAFF AND CONSULTANTS

Chapter 29
DEALING WITH DISAPPROVED OR OBSOLETE MOTIONS

Chapter 30

TO THE READER

This book has been described as "Robert's rules of order without the deadwood." It's an apt description.

The term "Robert's rules of order" is commonly used today as a synonym for parliamentary procedure. When people say a meeting is to be held according to Robert's rules, they generally mean only that it will be conducted with some formality—that proposals will be presented as motions and will be seconded and voted upon.

The term originated, of course, with a book published by General Henry Robert in 1876, originally entitled *Pocket Manual of Rules of Order for Deliberative Assemblies.* The book is now generally recognized as obsolete, embodying a number of cumbersome procedures and archaic terms, although its basic rules, based on the practices of Congress, are sound. In 1970 General Robert's daughter-in-law, Sarah Corbin Robert, recognizing the need for a replacement for the original volume, wrote a book entitled *Robert's Rules of Order Newly Revised.* It was, she said, "rewritten and enlarged to become essentially a new book, with a new title." Unfortunately, it retained all of the archaic procedures and terminology of the old one. (It was definitely enlarged, however—the most recent edition of the "pocket manual" has more than 700 pages!)

Neither General Robert's book nor that of his heirs meets the needs of today's fast-paced society, because the modern meeting-goer has no desire to master the intricacies of parliamentary law as practiced in the nineteenth century. Most organizations today, even though they may still list Robert's rules as their authority, simply ignore the more burdensome provisions, such as the complex limitations on reconsideration or the quaint ritual of the "committee of the whole."

When controversy arises, however, the rules cannot be ignored—and that's when the trouble starts, with a knowledgeable minority using the rules to thwart the will of the assembly.

A good example of deadwood is General Robert's motion to reconsider and enter on the minutes, the so-called "monkey-wrench" motion. This arcane procedure enables two people (one to make the motion and another to second it) to circumvent the will of an entire assembly—and without a vote! True, it is rarely used, but that is only because so few people are aware of it. Whenever it is used it causes bitterness and acrimony, violating, as it does, the principle of majority rule.

Alice Sturgis believed that confusing or unnecessary motions and terminology should be eliminated. Her goal was to make the process simpler, fairer, and easier to understand, and *The Standard Code of Parliamentary Procedure* did just that, preserving the traditional procedures, but—to borrow a phrase from the computer industry—making them more "user-friendly."

Since the publication of the third edition of the *Standard Code* in 1988, many organizations have changed their bylaws to designate it as their parliamentary authority, and many readers have found that it helped them better understand the process of democratic decision making. I hope that you, too, will find it . . . well, user-friendly!

Edwin C. Bliss
Chairman
AIP Revision Committee

INTRODUCTION

In the foreword to the second edition of the *Sturgis Standard Code of Parliamentary Procedure*, Erwin N. Griswold, Dean of the Harvard University Law School, said:

> In this volume, the author has presented in clear terms an exposition of standard parliamentary procedures. Instead of a skeleton in the form of a mere "code" or "rules," she has put flesh on the bones, with clear explanations, illustrations, and illuminating comments. A presiding officer who uses this book can conduct a fair and effective meeting, can make sound rulings, and will be in a position to maintain the rulings if they are challenged. Many books on parliamentary law have been published in the past. Some of them are classics of their period, such as *Jefferson's Manual, Cushing's Manual,* and *Robert's Rules of Order.* But these are often technical, cryptic and really intelligible only to specialists. Moreover, they are dated, and do not reflect current practices with full accuracy. This book has the great merit of combining clarity and readability with sound and well-conceived procedures appropriate to the present time.

In the two decades since those words were written, this book has helped countless people to master the principles by which meetings are conducted in a democratic society. In keeping with Alice Sturgis's desire that the book always reflect the most current practices, the publishers asked the American Institute of Parliamentarians to recommend changes for the third edition.

Revision has been kept to a minimum, as befits a book which has been so well received. Except for changes in wording for greater clarity or to minimize gender bias, the only major changes have been the elimination of two rarely used motions—to postpone indefinitely and object to consideration—and the validation of the almost universal practice of suppressing a motion by "tabling" it. Some purists have objected to this use of the motion to table, since the motion is undebatable, and thus permits a bare majority to suppress a motion without allowing discussion of it. Nevertheless, tabling continues to be the most popular way of setting a motion aside permanently. To legitimize the practice, while at the same time protecting against abuse, the *Standard Code* now requires a two-thirds vote for passage of the motion to table whenever its purpose is to kill a motion without discussion instead of merely to postpone its consideration.

With the acceptance of tabling as a valid way of suppressing a question, the motion to postpone indefinitely no longer is needed. Although this motion was seldom heard in the ordinary assembly, it was in *Robert's Rules* and most other parliamentary manuals, and was always a potential source of trouble, available to confuse less sophisticated members and presiding officers. Its very name was misleading—its purpose was not to "postpone," but to kill. It was sometimes used to circumvent the rule against a straw vote; but in such cases its use was unfair because it provided a nonbinding test vote for opponents of the measure while denying such an opportunity to proponents. Postpone indefinitely also was used as a way of getting around a limitation on the number of times a member could speak on a motion, because theoretically it presented a new question, although actually it did not. When additional time for debate is needed, the correct procedure is to ask the assembly to grant more time, instead of resorting to devious tactics and gamesmanship.

The elimination of game playing, in fact, is what the *Standard Code* is all about. It was Alice Sturgis's view that respect for the democratic process could grow only if the process was understandable and straightforward. She despised the arcane phrases and circuitous tactics that often cause a meeting to degenerate into a parliamentary sparring contest among "experts," leaving the bulk of the audience bewildered.

An example of the game playing Mrs. Sturgis deplored is the practice of voting contrary to one's belief in order to be able to move to reconsider, as was necessary under *Robert's Rules of Order* and other older parliamentary authorities. Alice Sturgis believed, as do many modern experts, that such gimmickry has no place in a democratic assembly, and that anyone should be permitted to move that a vote be reconsidered.

The motion to reconsider, incidentally, is a good example of the contrast between the *Standard Code* and some of the older parliamentary manuals. Under the *Standard Code* the rule is simple: a main motion may be reconsidered; other motions may not. In *Robert's Rules of Order Newly Revised,* however, the explanation of this motion requires twenty pages, with twenty-five motions that can be reconsidered, and twenty-five motions that cannot be reconsidered. Then there are twenty motions on which a negative vote can be reconsidered, but an affirmative vote cannot, and one on which an affirmative vote can be reconsidered, but a negative vote cannot.[1] This labyrinthine tangle of rules and restrictions is incomprehensible to the average meeting-goer. It is easy to see why one parliamentary procedure study group devoted all of its meetings for an entire year to a study of Robert's motion to reconsider!

The elimination of archaic or troublesome procedures does not, of course, mean that they will not be encountered, because many people are accustomed to using them. To ensure that anyone using this book will understand how to deal with such situations, a separate chapter has been added on handling of discontinued motions (Chapter 29, Dealing with Disapproved or Obsolete Motions). A chapter on often-asked questions (Chapter 30) also has been added, intended especially to aid persons unfamiliar with parliamentary procedure.

Those of us who have worked on the third edition of this classic volume have tried constantly to keep in mind the philosophy of its original author. Alice Sturgis considered principles more important than rules; she stressed the need to understand the "why" behind every procedure; and she held that when there is a conflict between common sense and archaic ritual, common sense should prevail.

We believe she was right, and we trust this revision will reflect that belief.

Revision Committee
American Institute of Parliamentarians

Chapter 1

THE SIGNIFICANCE
OF PARLIAMENTARY LAW

> Procedure is more than formality. Procedure is, indeed, the great mainstay of substantive rights....Without procedural safeguards—liberty would rest on precarious ground and substantive rights would be imperiled.
> *William O. Douglas[1]*

> The history of liberty has largely been the history of observance of procedural safeguards.
> *Felix Frankfurter[2]*

Thus two justices of the Supreme Court of the United States voice this vital fact—both our freedom and our rights can exist only if they are safeguarded by sound procedures, rigidly enforced.

Parliamentary Law Safeguards Rights

When Winston Churchill, during the abdication crisis in 1936, rose before a shocked House of Commons to discuss the constitutional question before a final decision was made, the House was in a hostile temper. A burst of disapproval greeted the great statesman. Churchill set his pugnacious jaw and, as the uproar subsided, declared:

"If the House resists my claim [to speak] it will only add more importance to any words that I may use."

Here in the mother of parliaments, which has lent its name to the system of rules by which assemblies are conducted, we see at work procedural safeguards and the fundamental principles of democratic discussion. Here is the right of free and fair debate, the right of the majority to decide, and the right of the minority to protest and be protected. Here also is a demonstra-

1

tion that the violation of rights in assemblies lends weight to the cause of the suppressed.

Here is the essence of the democratic procedure of a free assembly, whether a professional society, a political organization, a labor union, or a social club—a procedure based on what Thomas Jefferson called "equal and exact justice to all."

Any right is only as strong as the procedures that enforce it. To vote by secret ballot is a fundamental right, but it is meaningless unless supported by procedures that ensure equal opportunity to vote, freedom of choice, absolute secrecy, and honesty in counting. Even though this right to vote has procedural safeguards, it still is meaningless if they are not observed.

Parliamentary law is the procedural safeguard that protects the individual and the group in their exercise of the rights of free speech, free assembly, and the freedom to unite in organizations for the achievement of common aims. These rights, too, are meaningless, and the timeless freedoms they define can be lost, if parliamentary procedure is not observed.

One of the basic concepts of freedom is the right of people to join together to achieve their common purposes. This concept includes the right to assemble and to organize, to propose ideas, to speak without fear of reprisal, to vote on proposals, and to carry out the decisions of the group. Parliamentary law provides the procedures that give reality to these democratic concepts. Parliamentary procedure is not an end in itself. It is, rather, the guardian of the freedom to band together, to discuss, to decide, and to act.

What Is Parliamentary Law?

Parliamentary law is the code of rules and ethics for working together in groups. It has evolved through centuries out of the experience of individuals working together for a common purpose. It provides the means of translating beliefs and ideas into effective group action. It is logic and common sense crystallized into law, and is as much a part of the body of the law as is civil or criminal procedure. The rules of parliamentary procedure are found both in common law and in statutory law.

The common law of parliamentary procedure is the body of principles, rules, and usages that has developed from court decisions on parliamentary questions, and is based on reason and long observance. The common law of parliamentary procedure applies in all parliamentary situations except where a statutory law governs.

The statutory law of procedure consists of statutes, or law, relating to procedures that have been enacted by federal, state, or local legislative bodies. These rules of parliamentary procedure apply only to the particular organizations covered by the law.

Parliamentary procedure is easy to learn, because it is essentially fairness and common sense. It gives confidence and power to those who master it, and it enables members and organizations to present, consider, and carry out their ideas with efficiency and harmony.

It is true that parliamentary law can be used to obstruct the will of the majority, as well as to implement it—but this can happen only when a majority of the members are ignorant of their parliamentary rights.

What Organizations Must Observe Parliamentary Law?

Deliberative bodies, such as business, cultural, religious, social, fraternal, professional, educational, labor, civic, scientific, medical, and governmental organizations, are subject to the principles of common parliamentary law. All profit and nonprofit corporations and associations, and the boards, councils, commissions, and committees of government, must observe its rules.

International and national parliaments, congresses, and state legislatures have developed complete sets of special rules to meet their own specialized needs, and most of these rules differ sharply from those of common parliamentary law. Therefore, these bodies are not subject to common parliamentary law.

Clarence Cannon, former member of Congress and parliamentarian of the House of Representatives, explains why the rules of Congress are not suitable for other bodies to use:

> These rules of Parliament and Congress are designed for bicameral bodies, generally with paid memberships, meet-

ing in continuous session, requiring a majority for a quorum, and delegating their duties largely to committees. Their special requirements...have produced highly complex and remarkably efficient systems of rules peculiar to their respective bodies, but which are, as a whole, unsuited to the needs of the ordinary assembly.[3]

When Must Organizations Observe Parliamentary Law?

The courts hold that all deliberative groups, with the exception of state, national, and international governmental bodies, must follow general parliamentary law whenever they are meeting to transact business. If, however, a group meets solely for other purposes—for example, social or educational—it is, of course, not subject to parliamentary rules.

Even a small group—for example, a finance committee or a board of education—must observe parliamentary law. However, the procedure in such groups is usually more informal than in a large convention.

When a group meets for the purpose of presenting proposals, discussing them, and arriving at democratic decisions, parliamentary procedure is not only helpful, but indispensable. In all organizations the rules of procedure must be observed if the actions of the assembly are to be legal.

Where Parliamentary Rules Are Found

The four basic sources of the parliamentary rules governing a particular organization, arranged in the order of their rank, are:

1. Law. The law, consisting of the common law of parliamentary procedure and the statutes enacted by federal, state, or local governments, is the highest source of parliamentary rules for any organization.

2. Charter. The charter granted by government to an incorporated organization ranks second as a source. The charter granted by a parent organization to a constituent or component unit of the organization ranks next to its charter from government.

3. Bylaws. Any provisions of the bylaws of a parent organization that regulate the constituent or component units of the organization rank ahead of the bylaws adopted by the units. The bylaws, or the constitution and bylaws, and other adopted rules of an organization rank next.

4. Adopted parliamentary authority. The book adopted by an organization as its authority on all procedural questions *not* covered by the law or its charters, bylaws, or adopted rules completes the sources of the parliamentary rules governing an organization. A parliamentary authority is a compilation of the parliamentary rules from *all of these sources,* assembled and organized for convenient reference.

A parliamentary authority suited for adoption (*a*) explains the principles and procedures that are based on long-time parliamentary usages and accepted practices; (*b*) summarizes and interprets the common law of parliamentary procedure as determined by court decisions and the law contained in statutes applicable to particular organizations; and (*c*) presents practical ideas developed by leading organizations for efficient operation.

If there is a conflict between sources, the higher-ranking source prevails. For example, a charter must not conflict with the law; bylaws must not conflict with either the law or charter.

Organizations also have the right to adopt rules that supplement or change the less fundamental provisions of parliamentary procedure. None of these adopted rules may conflict with any rule of higher rank. For example, a voluntary organization cannot adopt a rule requiring six months' notice for a resignation, because common law gives a member the right to resign at any time.

Requirements for a Parliamentary Authority

Each organization adopts, as a parliamentary authority, a code that governs the procedures of the organization in all situations not covered by rules from a higher source. Because of its importance to the organization, the parliamentary authority should be chosen with great care.

A parliamentary authority should be so clear and simple that anyone can understand it. It should be organized so that reference to the rules is quick and accurate, and it should be so complete that no other book or research will be needed. It should omit needless or outmoded procedures but must include all current, practical, businesslike procedures. It must present parliamentary law so accurately that the courts will uphold any action taken according to the rules it states. If the rules of the adopted parliamentary authority do not conform to the law, the organization that follows it may find itself in legal difficulties.

This *Standard Code* has been written to meet these standards, drawing its strength and completeness from the broad experience and sound judgment of leaders in many fields. It is truly a cooperative effort, for it embodies and reflects the experience and wisdom of hundreds of organizations and innumerable individuals. These leaders and organizations have contributed to this code because of their conviction that voluntary organizations are the highest fulfillment of democracy.

Chapter 2

FUNDAMENTAL PRINCIPLES
OF PARLIAMENTARY LAW

A knowledge of the basic principles of parliamentary law enables one to reason out the answers to most parliamentary questions. A thorough understanding of these principles clarifies the entire subject of parliamentary procedure. When one understands the basic principles, it is easy to become familiar with the rules because most of them follow logically from the principles.

These basic principles are so simple and familiar that we may fail to recognize their importance. They are the same principles on which democracies are based and seem almost self-evident.

The most important principles of parliamentary procedure are those that follow.

The Purpose of Parliamentary Law

The purpose of parliamentary procedure is to facilitate the transaction of business and to promote cooperation and harmony. The philosophy of parliamentary law is constructive—to make it easier for people to work together effectively and to help organizations and members accomplish their purposes.

Parliamentary procedure should not be used to awe, entangle, or confound the uninitiated. Technical rules should be used only to the extent necessary to observe the law, to expedite business, to avoid confusion, and to protect the rights of members.

Two basic procedural rules have developed to assure that the simplest and most direct procedure for accomplishing a purpose is observed. First, motions have a definite order of precedence, each motion having a fixed rank for its introduction and its consideration. Second, only one motion may be considered at a time.

Equality of Rights

All members have equal rights, privileges, and obligations. Every member has an equal right to propose motions, speak, ask questions, nominate, be a candidate for office, vote, or exercise any other privilege of a member. Every member also has equal obligations.

The presiding officer should be strictly impartial and should act promptly to protect the equality of members in the exercise of their rights and privileges.

Majority Decision

The majority vote decides. The ultimate authority of an organization is vested in a majority of its members. This is a fundamental concept of democracy.

A primary purpose of parliamentary procedure is to determine the will of the majority and see that it is carried out. By the act of joining a group, a member agrees to be governed by the vote of the majority. Until the vote on a question is announced, every member has an equal right to voice opposition or approval and to seek to persuade others. After the vote is announced, the decision of the majority becomes the decision of every member of the organization. It is the duty of every member to accept and to abide by this decision.

When the members of an organization select officers, boards, or sometimes committees, and delegate authority to them, this selection and delegation should be by the democratic process of majority vote.

Minority Rights

The rights of the minority must be protected. Democratic organizations always protect certain basic rights belonging to all members. The right to present proposals, to be heard, and to oppose are valued rights of all members, although the ultimate authority of decision rests with a majority, except when a higher vote is required. The members who are in the minority on a question are entitled to the same consideration and respect as members who are in the majority.

The minority of today is frequently the majority of tomorrow. A member of the majority on one question may be in the minority on the next. The protection of the rights of all members, minority and majority alike, should be the concern of every member.

The Right of Discussion

Full and free discussion of every proposition presented for decision is an established right of members. Each member of the assembly has the right to speak freely without interruption or interference provided the rules are observed. The right of members to "have their say," or to "have their day in court," is as important as their right to vote.

The Right to Information

Every member has the right to know the meaning of the question before the assembly and what its effect will be. The presiding officer should keep the pending motion clearly before the assembly at all times, and when necessary should explain it or call on some member to do so. Any motion and its effect should be explained if there are members who do not understand it. Members have the right to request information on any motion they do not understand so that they may vote intelligently.

Fairness and Good Faith

All meetings must be characterized by fairness and by good faith. Trickery, overemphasis on minor technicalities, dilatory tactics, indulgence in personalities, and railroading threaten the spirit and practice of fairness and good faith. If a meeting is characterized by fairness and good faith, a minor procedural error will not invalidate an action that has been taken by an organization. But fraud, unfairness, or absence of good faith may cause a court to hold any action invalid.

Parliamentary strategy is the art of using legitimately the parliamentary principles, rules, and motions to support or defeat a proposal. It includes, for example, such important factors as timing, wording of proposals, choice of supporters, selection of arguments, and manipulation of proposals by other motions. Strategy, ethically used, is constructive; however, if it involves deceit, fraud, misrepresentation, intimidation, railroading, or denial of the rights of members, it is destructive and actually illegal.

In 1776 John Hatsell, the famous British parliamentarian, wrote, "Motives ought to outweigh objections of form." The interpretations of the courts make it clear that the intent and overall good faith of the group are of more importance than the particular detail of procedure used in a given instance. The effectiveness and, in fact, often the existence of an organization are destroyed if its officers or members condone unfairness or lack of good faith.

Chapter 3

PRESENTATION OF MOTIONS

Steps in Presenting a Motion

A *motion* is the formal statement of a proposal or question to an assembly for consideration and action. An item of business is presented for decision in the form of a main motion, also referred to as a "question" or "proposition." Presenting a motion requires the following steps:

1. A member rises and addresses the presiding officer.

2. The member is recognized by the presiding officer.

3. The member proposes the motion.

4. Another member seconds the motion.

5. The presiding officer states the motion to the assembly.

Addressing the Presiding Officer

Any member has the right to present a motion. To do this, he or she rises and addresses the presiding officer using the appropriate title, such as "Madam President," or "Mr. Chairman," or "Madam Moderator." If the member does not know the official title of the presiding officer, the terms "Mr. Chairman" or "Madam Chairman" are always correct, unless the organization has adopted a different style of address.* Addressing the pre-

* See p. 236.

siding officer indicates that the member wishes to obtain the floor, that is, to have the right to present a motion or to speak. After addressing the presiding officer, the member waits for recognition.

Recognition by the Presiding Officer

The presiding officer may recognize a member by calling the member's name. If the presiding officer does not know the member's name, some other designation may be used, such as "the delegate at the microphone in the center aisle," or the chair may nod to the person or use another appropriate form of recognition. In large organizations and conventions it is advisable to establish a policy at the beginning of a meeting for members, when recognized, to identify themselves by name, and, if appropriate, the state, district, or other unit they represent.

It is traditional in parliamentary procedure for members to address each other by last names, even though they may ordinarily be on a first-name basis. In a large group, especially, this adds a note of formality, which keeps the discussion on a higher plane. In recent years, however, with the trend toward greater informality, this practice is often ignored, especially in small groups and in social organizations where all members are on a first-name basis. Under no circumstances, however, should the chair call some members by their first names and others by their last, as this creates the feeling of an "in-group," composed of close friends of the presiding officer, and an "out-group" of comparative strangers.

In very large assemblies it is often the custom to avoid the use of names altogether, as much as possible, referring to members by such terms as "the previous speaker," or "the maker of the motion," or "the delegate from Arizona." This helps to keep discussion impersonal, and is especially recommended in conventions, where one speaks not as an individual but as a representative of a chapter or other constituency.

Having received formal recognition from the presiding officer, a member is said to have the floor and is entitled to present a motion or to speak. Other members who were also seeking recognition should be seated as soon as one member is recognized.

Proposal of a Motion by a Member

A motion must be stated in the form "I move that...," which means "I propose that...," followed by a statement of the proposal which the member wishes to bring before the assembly, for example: "I move that this organization purchase a site for a new headquarters building."

The enacting clause "I move..." is the only correct wording for introducing a motion. It gives notice to the presiding officer and to the assembly that the speaker is submitting a proposal for decision. Awkward forms such as "I move you" or "I make a motion that" are incorrect. Statements beginning "I propose" or "I suggest" should not be recognized as motions. The presiding officer should inquire of the member making such a statement, "Do you wish to state your proposal as a motion?" Aside from an occasional brief explanatory remark, no discussion is permissible until the presiding officer states the motion to the assembly.

The proposer of a lengthy, complicated, or important motion should prepare written copies of it and give them to the presiding officer and to the secretary. The presiding officer may require that the maker of such a motion submit it in writing.

Seconding a Motion

After proposing the motion, the member sits down. Another member may, without waiting for recognition, say, "I second the motion" or just "Second." Seconding a motion merely indicates that the member wishes the motion to be considered by the assembly; it is not necessarily an endorsement of the motion.

If the motion is not seconded, the presiding officer inquires: "Is there a second to this motion?" A motion sometimes fails to receive a second because the meaning of the motion is not clear to the members. In such a case, the presiding officer should restate the motion more clearly and ask again if there is a second. If there is no response, the chair may declare: "Since there is no second, the motion is not before the assembly," and proceed to other business.

Routine motions, such as approving the minutes, are frequently put to vote without waiting for a second. If any member objects to the lack of a second, the presiding officer must call for one.

Statement of a Motion
by the Presiding Officer

When a motion has been properly moved and seconded, the presiding officer states it to the assembly. It is the duty of the presiding officer to state every motion as correctly and clearly as possible even though it may be necessary to change the wording of the motion. The meaning of the motion, however, cannot be changed without the consent of its proposer. If the presiding officer makes an error in stating a motion, or if there is a difference of opinion as to the exact wording of a motion, the motion as stated by the member is the legal motion.

The presiding officer states the motion as follows: "It has been moved and seconded that this organization establish a summer camp for its members and their families" or "It has been moved and seconded that the following resolution be adopted: '*Resolved,* That this congregation commend the courageous action of our minister at the International Religious Council.'"

As soon as a motion has been stated to the assembly by the presiding officer, it is open for discussion if it is debatable. From the time a motion is stated by the presiding officer until it is disposed of, it is called a "pending question" or "pending motion."

Example of the Presentation of a Motion

MR. A (*rising and addressing the presiding officer*): "Mr. President."

PRESIDING OFFICER: "Mr. A."

MR. A: "I move that this organization undertake a campaign to raise funds for the purchase of the property to the north of our clubhouse."

MR. B (*without rising*): "I second the motion."

PRESIDING OFFICER: "It has been moved and seconded that this organization undertake a campaign to raise funds for the purchase of the Beekman property. Is there any discussion?...

"Those in favor of the motion that this organization undertake a campaign to raise funds for the purchase of the Beekman property say 'Aye.'...Those opposed, 'No.'...The motion is carried."

Chapter 4

CLASSIFICATION OF MOTIONS

Classes of Motions

Motions are classified, according to their purposes (page 266) and characteristics, into four groups:

Main motions

Subsidiary motions

Privileged motions

Incidental motions

Main Motions

Main motions are the most important and most frequently used. The main motion is the foundation of the conduct of business. Its purpose is to bring substantive proposals before the assembly for consideration and action. After it is stated by the presiding officer, the main motion becomes the subject for deliberation and decision.

There are three main motions that have specific names and are governed by somewhat different rules. They are referred to as "*specific* main motions" to distinguish them from *the* main motion. The most frequently used specific main motions are:

Reconsider

Rescind

Resume consideration (take from the table)

Subsidiary Motions

Subsidiary motions alter the main motion, or delay or hasten its consideration. Consequently, they are subsidiary to it. Subsidiary motions are usually applied to the main motion but some of them may be applied to certain other motions.

The most frequently used subsidiary motions are:

Postpone temporarily (lay on the table)

Close debate (previous question)

Limit debate

Postpone definitely

Refer to a committee

Amend

Privileged Motions

Privileged motions have no direct connection with the main motion before the assembly. They are motions of such urgency that they are entitled to immediate consideration. They relate to the members and to the organization rather than to particular items of business. Privileged motions would be main motions but for their urgency. Because of their urgency, they are given the privilege of being considered ahead of other motions that are before the assembly.

The privileged motions are:

Adjourn

Recess

Question of privilege

Incidental Motions

Incidental motions arise only incidentally out of the business before the assembly. They do not relate directly to the main motion, but usually relate to matters incidental to the conduct of the meeting. Incidental motions may be offered whenever they are needed, and have no order of precedence. Because of their very nature they may interrupt business and in some cases may interrupt the speaker, and should be handled as soon as they arise.

Incidental motions include:

Appeal from a decision of the chair

Consider informally

Suspend the rules

Point of order

Parliamentary inquiry

Withdrawal of a motion

Division of a question

Division of the assembly

The first three listed, appeal, consider informally, and suspend the rules, are motions, and therefore require a second, and are decided by a vote of the assembly. Point of order, parliamentary inquiry, withdrawal of a motion, division of a question, and division of the assembly, although technically classified as motions, are actually requests, to be handled or decided by the presiding officer. Two of these requests, withdrawal of a motion and division of a question, if not granted by the presiding officer, may be presented as motions for decision by vote of the assembly.

Classification of Unlisted Motions

The motions within each class—main, subsidiary, privileged, and incidental—differ somewhat but have similar purposes and characteristics. Only the more commonly used motions in each class are listed in charts and classifications. There are many other motions that may be proposed, and the presiding officer must know how to classify them in order to determine whether they are in order and what rules govern them. Therefore, it is essential to understand the purposes and characteristics of each class in order to classify the less used motions.

For example, while a main motion is being considered, a member might move "that the vote on the motion be taken by roll call." This might appear to be a main motion. It is, however, an incidental motion because it arises incidentally out of the business before the assembly. It would therefore be in order and would be decided immediately. Or a member might move "that the article in tonight's *Tribune* explaining the reason for the tax raise we are considering be procured and read to the assembly." This would be a privileged motion because of its urgency and would be considered immediately. Without an understanding of the classification of motions, the presiding officer might mistakenly think that the examples just cited are main motions and rule them out of order on the ground that another main motion is pending.

The name given a motion by its proposer is not the determining factor in classifying the motion, because the proposer may name the motion incorrectly. For example, someone might move "to postpone the motion temporarily until ten o'clock." This is a motion to *postpone definitely*, not to *postpone temporarily*, since a time is specified.

Changes in Classification of Motions

A motion that usually is listed in one classification may belong in another if it is proposed in a different situation. The classification of a motion usually is based on the relationship of that motion to the main motion. The main motion is the foundation motion that determines the classification of other motions.

Usually a main motion is already pending when a subsidiary, privileged, or incidental motion is proposed. But certain of the subsidiary, privileged, or incidental motions may be proposed when no main motion is pending. In this situation they are classified as main motions.

The following subsidiary, privileged, and incidental motions (with an example of a possible form in which each might be proposed) may be proposed as main motions when no main motion is pending.

Subsidiary Motions

Limit debate. "I move that debate on the proposed assessment, scheduled to come up at three o'clock this afternoon, be limited to one hour."

Postpone definitely. "I move that all the reports of special committees be postponed until Friday evening."

Refer to committee. "I move that we create a committee on insurance and refer to it the investigation of additional benefits."

Amend (if applied to an action already taken). "I move to amend the motion passed on January 3 'that the president appoint three members to act as a committee to arrange a seminar on foreign relations' by adding the words 'and that the membership elect two additional members.'"

Privileged Motions

Adjourn. "I move we adjourn," or "I move we adjourn this evening promptly at nine o'clock so that we may attend the hearings of the reference committees."

Recess. "I move that we recess for five minutes," or "I move that we recess for lunch as soon as the finance report is presented."

Question of privilege (presented as a motion). "I move that the author of the Survey on Fire Protection be asked to come this afternoon to answer questions on his report."

Incidental Motions

Appeal. PRESIDING OFFICER: "Your request to make a brief presentation of your idea for increasing the membership is out of order since no motion is pending." MEMBER: "I appeal from the decision of the chair."

Suspend rules. "I move that we suspend the rules prohibiting speeches by guests during business meetings so that when we meet tonight the mayor may speak on the plan for garbage disposal."

Chapter 5

PRECEDENCE OF MOTIONS

Order of Precedence

Precedence means the priority or order in which motions must be proposed, considered, and disposed of. The purpose of assigning a rank or order to each commonly used motion is to enable an assembly to propose, consider, and decide each motion without confusion. From the highest ranking to the lowest ranking the order of precedence is:

Privileged Motions

1. Adjourn

2. Recess

3. Question of privilege

Subsidiary Motions

4. Postpone temporarily (or table)

5. Close debate

6. Limit debate

7. Postpone definitely

8. Refer to committee

9. Amend

Main Motions

10. The main motion and specific main motions

Incidental motions have no order of precedence. Since they arise incidentally out of the immediately pending business at any time and must be decided as soon as they arise, they present no problem of precedence.

Basic Rules of Precedence

There are two basic rules of precedence:

1. When a motion is being considered, any motion of higher precedence may be proposed, but no motion of lower precedence may be proposed. For example, when a main motion (10) is pending, a member may move to refer the motion to a committee (8). Another member may move to recess (2). There will then be three motions pending at the same time. Since the proper order of precedence was followed in proposing them, there will be no confusion in considering and disposing of them.

2. Motions are considered and voted on in reverse order to their proposal. The motion last proposed is considered and disposed of first. For example, if motions (10), (8), and (2) are proposed in that order and are pending, they are considered and decided in the reverse order, which is (2), (8), and (10).

Example of Precedence

Suppose that a member proposes a main motion (10) "that all members of the Chamber of Commerce be assessed five dollars for the Christmas Fund." While this motion is pending, another member moves to amend it by striking out the word "five" and inserting the word "ten" (9). While this amendment is being discussed, someone moves to "limit debate on the amendment to one speech per person of no more than three minutes" (6).

Then another member moves to postpone the motion until the next meeting (7). Immediately, a member rises to a point of order (an incidental motion, which can be made whenever necessary), and calls attention to the fact that the motion to postpone definitely (7) is out of order because it is of lower precedence than the immediately pending question (6). The presiding officer rules the member's point "well taken" and declares the motion to postpone definitely out of order, stating that the immediately pending question is the motion to limit debate. A member then moves "that we take a recess" (2).

All these motions, except the one ruled out of order, have followed correct precedence and are therefore in order. The following four motions are pending:

Motions Pending	*Order of Precedence*
Recess	2
Limit debate	6
Amend	9
The main motion	10

The presiding officer first takes a vote on the motion to recess. If it loses, the chair calls for a vote on the motion to limit debate. After that motion has been carried or defeated, the motion to amend is the immediately pending question. After it has been discussed and voted on, the chair calls for discussion on the main motion.

While the assembly is considering one of the four motions in this chain of precedence, a member may present another motion, provided it has a higher precedence than the one that is being considered. For example, while the motion to limit debate is pending, a motion to close debate would be in order, but a motion to refer to committee would not.

Complicated problems of precedence occur only rarely. Quite frequently, however, two or three motions are awaiting decision by the assembly. All motions that have been proposed and stated to the assembly but are not yet decided are called *pending questions* or *pending motions*.

The particular motion being considered by the assembly at any particular time is called the *immediately pending motion* (or *question*).

Chapter 6

RULES GOVERNING MOTIONS

The Basic Rules of Motions

Rules governing motions are definite and logical. If you understand the purpose of a motion, you can usually reason out the rules governing it.

The rules or facts that you need to know about each motion are:

1. What is the precedence of the motion?

2. Can the motion interrupt a speaker?

3. Does the motion require a second?

4. Is the motion debatable?

5. Can the motion be amended?

6. What vote does the motion require?

7. To what other motions can the motion apply?

8. What other motions can be applied to the motion?

What Is the Precedence of the Motion?

To avoid confusion, each motion is assigned a definite rank. This rank is based on the urgency of the motion. Motions are listed in the order of their precedence on pages 264–265. When a motion is before the assembly, any motion is in order if it has a higher precedence or rank than the immediately pending motion, but no motion having a lower precedence is in order. Motions are considered and decided in reverse order to that of their proposal.

Can the Motion Interrupt a Speaker?

Two types of motions, because of their urgency, can interrupt a speaker. The first are those motions that must be proposed and decided within a specific time limit: to reconsider, to appeal, and division of the assembly. The motion to reconsider must be made during the same meeting or convention at which the vote to be reconsidered was taken. An appeal and a call for division of the assembly must be made before other business intervenes.

The second are those motions that relate to the immediate rights and privileges of a member or of the assembly: question of privilege, point of order, and parliamentary inquiry. A question of privilege involving the immediate convenience, comfort, or rights of the organization or of its members is frequently so urgent that it justifies interrupting a speaker. A point of order involving a mistake, error, or failure to comply with the rules can interrupt a speaker if it relates to the speaker, or to some error that cannot await the completion of the speech for its determination. To justify interrupting a speaker a parliamentary inquiry must relate to the speaker, to the speech, or to some other matter that cannot be delayed until the completion of the speech.

Does the Motion Require a Second?

All motions require seconds except in meetings of committees, boards, or governmental bodies. To justify the consideration of the assembly, a proposal should have the support of at least two members: one who makes the motion and another, the seconder, who indicates a desire to have the proposal considered.

A few motions do not require seconds because, although technically classified as motions, actually they are *requests* that are decided by the presiding officer. These are: point of order, parliamentary inquiry, withdraw a motion, division of a question, division of the assembly, and question of privilege. Questions of privilege and withdrawal of a motion are sometimes presented as motions instead of as requests, in which case they require seconds.

Is the Motion Debatable?

Some motions are open to full debate, others are open to restricted debate, and some are undebatable. The only motions that are *fully debatable* are: main motions, amendments to main motions, rescind, and appeal.

Main motions are debatable because they present substantive propositions requiring the consideration and decision of the organization. Amendments to debatable motions actually involve a part of the motion itself, and are therefore debatable. An appeal from a decision of the chair is debatable because the presiding officer should give reasons for the chair's decision and the member appealing has a right to present reasons for appealing that decision. The motion to rescind a main motion which was previously passed is debatable because it repeals an action taken earlier which was itself debatable.

Five motions are open to *restricted* debate: to recess, to postpone definitely, to refer to a committee, to limit debate, and to reconsider. Restricted debate means brief discussion confined to a few specific points, relative to the purpose of the motion itself. Thus, debate on the motion to recess is restricted to brief discussion of the advisability of the recess and its length. Debate on the motion to postpone definitely is restricted to discussion of the advisability of postponing, and of the time to which the matter would be postponed. Debate on the motion to refer to a committee is restricted to the advisability of referral, and to the selection, membership, and duties of the committee, or instructions to it. Debate on the motion to limit debate is restricted to the need for limitation and the type and time of limitation. Debate on the motion to reconsider is restricted to the reasons for reconsidering. None of the motions subject to restricted debate opens the main motion to debate.

All other motions are *undebatable* because they deal with simple procedural questions which should not need discussion.

Can the Motion Be Amended?

A simple test determines whether a motion can be amended. If the motion might have been put in another way that would be substantially different, then it is amendable. For example, the motion "I move we recess for ten minutes" could have been stated, "I move we recess for thirty minutes." The motion "I move that we limit debate on this question to one more speech on each side," could have been stated, "I move that we limit debate to two more speeches on each side." Such motions therefore are amendable.

On the other hand, if a change in the wording would make the motion a different kind of motion, it is not amendable. For example, to try to amend the motion to postpone temporarily by saying, "I move to postpone this matter until the next meeting," would make it a different kind of motion (to postpone definitely), so the amendment is out of order.

Some motions can be amended freely, some can be amended with restrictions, and some cannot be amended. The only motions that can be amended freely are main motions and amendments. Four motions can be amended only within restrictions: to recess, to limit debate, and to postpone definitely can be amended only as to time or manner of restriction; to refer to a committee can be amended only as to the method of selection, size, duties, or instructions to the committee.

What Vote Does the Motion Require?

Most motions require a majority vote. Some, however, require a two-thirds vote, such as those which limit the rights of members to propose, discuss, and decide proposals, including the motions to close debate, to limit debate, and to suspend the rules. An organization's bylaws may provide that certain other motions require a two-thirds vote. For example, most bylaws require a two-thirds vote to amend the bylaws, and in some states statutory law requires a two-thirds vote for an organization to buy, sell or lease real estate, or to mortgage property.

To What Other Motions
Can the Motion Apply?

A motion is said to apply to another motion when it is used to alter or dispose of or affect the original motion in some way. For example, if a main motion is being considered, and a member moves "to postpone definitely the consideration of the motion until Friday at three o'clock," the motion to postpone definitely "applies to" the main motion.

Specific main motions apply only to the main motion. Subsidiary motions apply to main motions. The motions to close debate and to limit debate apply to all debatable motions. The motion to amend applies to the main motion and to the motions to amend, to refer, to postpone definitely, to limit debate, to recess, and to adjourn. Privileged motions relate to the organization and the welfare and rights of its members rather than to particular items of business and therefore do not apply to any other motion. Incidental motions do not apply to other motions, except that the motion to withdraw applies to any motion, and division of the question applies to main motions.

What Other Motions
Can Be Applied to the Motion?

When a motion is being considered, it is important to know what other motions can be applied to it.

1. All motions can have the motion to withdraw applied to them.

2. All debatable motions can have the motions to close debate and to limit debate applied to them.

3. All motions that may be worded in more than one way, producing different results, can have the motion to amend applied to them.

4. The main motion can have all the subsidiary and specific main motions applied to it. Specific main motions can have no other motions applied to them, except that the motions to reconsider and to rescind may have the motions to close debate and to limit debate applied to them.

5. Privileged and incidental motions can have no other motion applied to them, except that the motion to recess may be amended, and an appeal may have the motion to close debate and the motion to limit debate applied to it.

In addition to the eight questions about each motion that have been summarized in this chapter and on pages 264–265, there are two procedural questions that should be understood: "When can a motion be renewed?" and "What procedures apply to main motions already voted on?"

When Can a Motion Be Renewed?

As a general rule, when a main motion has been voted on and lost, the same, or substantially the same, motion cannot be proposed again at the same meeting or convention.

Parliamentary law recognizes, however, that an assembly may change its mind, just as an individual may, and that some method must be provided for changing a decision which has been made.

In the case of a main motion—one which presents a substantive proposal to the assembly—the matter can be brought before the assembly again at the same meeting or convention by the motion *to reconsider*, which is discussed on p. 33. Approval of the motion to reconsider cancels the earlier vote and enables the assembly to discuss and amend the motion further, if desired, and to take another vote.

All motions that are procedural rather than substantive may be renewed at the discretion of the chair.

If the motion in question was adopted at an earlier meeting or convention it cannot be reconsidered. It may be *repealed*, however, by the motion *to rescind*, which nullifies the earlier decision. Unlike the motion to reconsider, the motion to rescind (or to repeal) has no time limit: it can be used at the same meeting at which the main motion was adopted, or at any future meeting.

If the motion was *rejected* at an earlier meeting or convention it may be renewed by being reintroduced.

A motion which has been carried also can be affected by a new main motion. *Repeal by implication* automatically results from the adoption of a motion that conflicts in whole or in part with another motion or motions previously adopted. The first motion is repealed only to the extent that its provisions cannot be reconciled with those of the new motion.

Members may be unaware of related motions previously adopted or may have overlooked them. Before a member proposes a new motion, it is good procedure to search the records for adopted motions with which the new motion might conflict. Such motions should be repealed when a new motion is adopted. Repeal by implication is intended to correct *inadvertent* conflicts, and not to be a blanket method for disposing of previously adopted motions without voting directly on their repeal.

Repeal by implication applies to any previously adopted motion, rule, or bylaw that is in conflict with a newly adopted motion, rule, or bylaw. If the new motion conflicts with a provision in a source of higher authority, for example a charter, it is out of order.

CHANGING MAIN MOTIONS
ALREADY VOTED ON

	MAY BE USED:	APPLIES TO:
Motion to reconsider	Only at same meeting or convention	Any main motion carried or lost
Motion to rescind	At any meeting or convention	Any main motion carried
Amend by new main motion	At any meeting or convention	Any main motion carried
Renew by new main motion	At any meeting or convention	Any main motion lost
Repeal or amend by implication	At any meeting or convention	Any main motion previously carried which conflicts with later main motion

Chapter 7

MAIN MOTIONS

THE MAIN MOTION

Purpose

To bring a proposal before an assembly for discussion and decision.

Form

PROPOSER: "I move that we undertake a drive for new members."

or

"I move the adoption of the following resolution:

"*Whereas* the New Jersey Chamber of Commerce is rapidly outgrowing its present quarters, and

"*Whereas* the rental cost for suitable quarters is high and available buildings are inconveniently located, therefore, be it

"*Resolved* that we build our own state headquarters and appropriate $165,000 from our reserve fund to start a building fund for this purpose."

or

"I move that we hold our Annual Aviation Show on Friday, November 10."

PRESIDING OFFICER (*after hearing a second*): "It has been moved and seconded that we hold our Annual Aviation Show on Friday, November 10. Is there any discussion?"

The Main Motion Defined

The main motion is the means by which a member may present a substantive proposal to the assembly for consideration and action. It is the basic motion for the transaction of business. Since only one subject can be considered at one time, the main motion can be proposed only when no other motion is before the assembly.

Phrasing the Main Motion

Since the main motion is a proposal of any action that a member wishes to recommend to the assembly, it is broad in scope and varies greatly in wording. It must be introduced by the words "I move." Otherwise, wide latitude in wording is permitted.

A motion should be concise and clear. If a member presents a motion that is confusing, unnecessarily long, or involved, the presiding officer should ask the proposer to rephrase the motion and, if necessary, should assist the member in doing so. The presiding officer can rephrase the motion only in wording that is approved by its proposer.

If a motion is long or complicated or controversial it is wise to submit it in writing. The chair has a right to insist that any motion be submitted in writing.

The proposer of a main motion may rephrase or withdraw the motion at any time before it is stated by the presiding officer to the assembly for consideration. After that it may be changed or withdrawn only with the permission of the assembly.

The main motion should be stated in the affirmative, since the negative form often confuses members in voting. If a motion is presented in the negative, the presiding officer may request that the proposer rephrase the motion; or the chair may rephrase it with the consent of the proposer.

For example, the motion "I move that we do not permit any member to remain on the Survey Committee who has not been present at three consecutive meetings and has not been excused" is more clearly stated affirmatively as "I move that any member of the Survey Committee who misses three consecutive meetings without excuse be dropped from the committee."

The Main Motion in Resolution Form

Main motions that express sentiments or are a formal statement of the opinions of the assembly are usually stated in the form of resolutions. This form is also used when the proposal is highly important, or is long and involved. A resolution should be in writing and is usually introduced in such a form as:

> "I move the adoption of the following resolution: 'Resolved, That this organization express its appreciation of the excellent service rendered by our retiring President during the past two years and, be it further
>
> 'Resolved, That we endorse him as a candidate for the National Executive Committee.'"

Often a resolution is prefaced by statements, each introduced by the word *whereas,* that state the reasons for the resolution. The statements contained in the whereases are of no legal effect and sometimes are the cause of disagreement. Members frequently attempt to debate and amend these prefacing statements, often to the neglect of the main resolution. The whereases are useful mainly when the organization plans to publish the resolution and wishes the reasons for its adoption to be read with it.

Discussion on the Main Motion

As soon as the main motion has been formally stated to the assembly by the presiding officer, it is open for debate. It cannot be debated before this formal statement unless a motion has been passed to discuss it informally. (See *Informal Consideration,* p. 120.) Discussion on the main motion must conform to the rules governing debate.

Disposition of the Main Motion

Whenever the main motion has been stated to an assembly by the presiding officer, some action must be taken on it and recorded in the minutes. The main motion may be decided by a vote approving or defeating it, or it may be disposed of by some other motion such as refer to a committee. No main motion can be simply ignored; definite action must be taken on it.

No main motion can be substituted for another main motion except that a new motion on the same subject may be offered as a substitute amendment to the main motion. (See *Amendment by Substitution of a New Motion,* p. 46.)

When a main motion has been acted on and lost, it cannot be renewed in the same or substantially the same words at the same meeting or convention, but it may be *reconsidered* at the same meeting or convention or presented as a new motion at a later meeting or convention.

Effect of Adopting the Main Motion

To commit the organization to the proposal stated by the motion and approved by vote of the assembly.

Rules Governing the Main Motion

1. Cannot interrupt a speaker

2. Requires a second

3. Is debatable because it presents a substantive proposal for consideration

4. Can be amended

5. Requires a majority vote

6. Takes precedence over no other motions

7. Applies to no other motion

8. Can have applied to it all subsidiary motions, specific main motions, and to withdraw

MOTION TO RECONSIDER

Purpose

To enable an assembly to set aside a vote on a main motion taken at the same meeting or convention and to consider the motion again as though no vote had been taken on it.

Form

PROPOSER: "I move to reconsider the vote by which the motion to enlarge our library was passed earlier this evening."

PRESIDING OFFICER (*after hearing a second*): 'It has been moved and seconded to reconsider the vote by which the motion to enlarge our library was passed earlier this evening. Will the secretary please read this motion?...Is there any discussion on the motion to reconsider this vote?...Those in favor of reconsidering the vote say 'Aye.'...Those opposed, 'No.'...The motion to reconsider is carried. The motion to enlarge our library, as read by the secretary, is again open for discussion."

What Votes Can Be Reconsidered?

Main motions are occasionally approved or disapproved under a misapprehension or without adequate information, and sometimes later events cause an assembly to change its mind.

The vote on any main motion, whether carried or lost, can be reconsidered at the same meeting or convention, except when something that cannot be undone has been done as a result of the vote; for example, when an affirmative vote has resulted in a contract, when money has been paid, or when a time limit has passed.

The motion to reconsider can be applied only to the main motion. The same result is accomplished for all other motions by more simple and direct means. Other motions that have *lost* can be proposed again or renewed as soon as, in the judgment of the presiding officer, the vote might result differently. (See *When Can a Motion Be Renewed?*, p. 28.) Other motions that have *carried* can be changed easily by procedural motions. For example, if a motion has been referred to a committee, it can be recalled; and if it has been postponed temporarily (laid on the table), it can be brought up again by a motion to resume consideration of it.

Proposal of the Motion to Reconsider

The motion to reconsider is a *specific* main motion and can be offered at any time during a meeting. It is unusual in that, unlike an ordinary main motion, it may be proposed even though other business is under consideration, and, if necessary, it may interrupt a speaker. Proposal of the motion to reconsider suspends any action provided for in the motion that is proposed for reconsideration until the motion to reconsider is decided. When a motion to reconsider is proposed and seconded while other business is pending, the presiding officer directs the secretary to record its proposal; but the motion to reconsider is not considered until the pending business has been handled. It is then considered and decided immediately. If the motion to reconsider is offered when no other business is pending, it is considered immediately.

Who Can Move to Reconsider?

In the past some authorities have permitted the motion to reconsider to be offered only by a person who voted on the prevailing side when the main motion was originally considered. The limitation has always caused chicanery and resentment, and as far back as 1844, Luther Cushing, the eminent lawyer and parliamentarian, insisted that "a motion to reconsider may be made at any time or by any member, precisely like any other motion."[1]

Modern usage[2] upholds Cushing's position: In the absence of a provision to the contrary in the organization's bylaws or in its parliamentary authority, the motion to reconsider may be offered by anyone.[3]

The argument for restricting the motion to those who had voted on the prevailing side was that this would avoid abuse of the motion, the presumption being that otherwise the motion might be used for dilatory purposes. The purpose of the limitation, however, was defeated because under such a rule:

1. Any member could vote on the prevailing side for the sole purpose of being eligible to move to reconsider.

2. Even if a member had failed to vote with the prevailing side, a vote could be changed just prior to the final announcement of the vote, making the member eligible to move reconsideration.

3. Except in case of a roll call it was impossible to determine accurately how anyone had voted.

4. In a ballot vote no one could be asked how he or she voted because the inquiry would violate the fundamental principle of secrecy in a ballot vote.

Instead of relying on this ineffective and troublesome limitation, it is better to permit anyone to offer the motion to reconsider when it appears justified, as when new facts have come to light, or when an error needs to be corrected, or when a hasty decision appears to have been made. If the chair considers the motion dilatory it can be ruled out of order—as is the case with any dilatory motion. If there is disagreement about whether the motion is dilatory the decision of the chair can be appealed, in which case the ultimate decision is made by the assembly, as it should be.

Debate on the Motion to Reconsider

The motion to reconsider is debatable, but debate is limited to reasons for reconsidering the motion. Debate on the main motion must wait until the assembly has voted to reconsider it.*

Since the proposal of the motion to reconsider suspends action on a motion that has already been voted on, the motion to reconsider should be decided immediately and cannot be postponed to a later meeting, as older practice sometimes permitted. (See *Reconsider and Enter on the Minutes*, p. 225.)

Effect of Adopting the Motion
to Reconsider

To cancel or wipe out a vote on a motion as completely as though it had never been taken and to bring that motion before the assembly for consideration as though it had never been voted on.

---

*Some parliamentary authorities in the past permitted unlimited discussion of the main motion itself during debate on reconsideration. However, this puts the assembly in the absurd position of (in effect) reconsidering the motion before deciding whether to reconsider it. Furthermore, such a practice thus puts the power to compel reconsideration effectively in the hands of anyone who moves to reconsider, whereas only the assembly itself, having once disposed of a matter, should have the right to open it up again to further consideration during the same meeting.

Rules Governing the Motion to Reconsider

1. Can interrupt proceedings

2. Requires a second

3. Is debatable

4. Cannot be amended

5. Requires a majority vote

6. Takes precedence over no other motions

7. Applies to votes on main motions taken at same meeting

8. Can have applied to it to close debate, to limit debate, and to withdraw

MOTION TO RESCIND

Purpose

To repeal (cancel, nullify, void) a main motion passed at a previous meeting.

Form

PROPOSER: "I move to rescind the motion passed at the meeting on June 1 opposing new school bonds."

PRESIDING OFFICER (*after hearing a second*): "It has been moved and seconded to rescind the motion passed June 1 opposing new school bonds. The secretary will please read the motion referred to....Is there any discussion?...Those in favor of rescinding the motion read by the secretary say 'Aye.'...Those opposed, 'No.'... The motion to rescind is carried. The motion that this organization go on record as opposed to the issuance of new school bonds is rescinded."

What Motions May Be Rescinded?

Any main motion that was passed, no matter how long before, may be rescinded unless as a result of the vote something has been done that the assembly cannot undo.

The motion to rescind, if passed, affects the present and future only, since it is not retroactive. For example, if a motion to fine tardy members were rescinded, no more fines would be imposed; but fines already collected would be retained and fines imposed before the motion was rescinded would still be collectible.

Vote Required to Rescind

A motion to rescind requires a majority vote. However, a motion that required more than a majority vote to pass can be rescinded only by the same vote that was required to approve it. Similarly, if notice to members was required for the consideration of a motion, the same notice is required for the consideration of a motion to rescind that motion.

Rescind and Expunge

The motion to expunge is occasionally combined with the motion to rescind, as, for example "I move to rescind the motion passed January 5 relating to...and to expunge this motion from the minutes."

When a motion is expunged, the secretary does not erase the motion from the minutes, but draws a line around it, and marks it "expunged by order of this assembly," gives the date of the expunging, and signs the notation. The expunged motion is not included in any minutes published thereafter. This motion is used only rarely, when the assembly desires to remove the motion from its public record. The motion to expunge requires a majority vote, whether used alone or combined with the motion to rescind.

Effect of Adoption
of the Motion to Rescind

To repeal, cancel, nullify, or void the motion from the date of the adoption of the motion to rescind.

Rules Governing the Motion to Rescind

1. Cannot interrupt a speaker

2. Requires a second

3. Is debatable and opens to debate the motion it proposes to rescind

4. Cannot be amended

5. Requires a majority vote

6. Takes precedence over no other motions

7. Applies to main motions previously adopted

8. Can have applied to it the motions to limit debate, to vote immediately, and to withdraw

MOTION TO RESUME CONSIDERATION
(Take from the Table)

Purpose

To enable an assembly to take up and consider a motion that was postponed temporarily (tabled) during the same meeting or convention.

Form

PROPOSER: "I move to resume consideration of the motion concerning the campaign for new members that was postponed temporarily earlier in this meeting," *or* "I move that the motion to...be taken from the table."

PRESIDING OFFICER *(after hearing a second)*: "It has been moved and seconded that we resume consideration of the motion on the proposed campaign for new members. The secretary will please read this motion....Those in favor of resuming consideration of the motion 'that this organization undertake a campaign for three hundred new members' say 'Aye.'...Opposed, 'No.'...The motion to resume consideration is carried, and the motion 'that this organization undertake a campaign for three hundred new members' is now open for discussion."

Limitations on the Motion
to Resume Consideration

The motion to resume consideration is a specific main motion that applies only to a main motion that has been postponed temporarily (tabled) at the current meeting or convention. Beyond the current meeting or convention, the temporarily postponed motion lapses and can be brought up only as a new main motion.

Precedence over Other Main Motions

The motion to resume consideration of a motion can be proposed only when no other motion is pending. However, it takes precedence over any other new main motion that another member may seek to present at the same time. If a member rises to move that consideration be resumed on a motion that has been postponed temporarily and the presiding officer recognizes someone else, the member should at once state that he has risen to move to resume consideration of a motion. The presiding officer will then give the member priority over others who wish to propose new main motions.

Adhering Motions
and Resuming Consideration

If the main motion that was postponed temporarily had subsidiary motions attached to it—for example, a motion to amend—these motions still adhere to it when consideration is resumed and must be disposed of in the usual order. If the motion to limit debate or to close debate has been passed before the main motion was postponed temporarily, these motions are still in effect when consideration is resumed.

Effect of Adoption of the Motion
to Resume Consideration

To place the original main motion again before the assembly in the same state as it was when it was postponed temporarily.

Rules Governing the Motion
to Resume Consideration

1. Cannot interrupt a speaker

2. Requires a second

3. Is not debatable

4. Cannot be amended

5. Requires a majority vote

6. Takes precedence over other new main motions only

7. Applies to any main motion that has been postponed temporarily (or tabled)

8. Can have applied to it no motion except the motion to withdraw

Chapter 8

SUBSIDIARY MOTIONS

MOTION TO AMEND

Purpose

To modify a motion that is being considered by the assembly so that it will express more satisfactorily the will of the members.

Form

Assume that the following motion is under consideration: "I move that this organization send representatives to the Council and to the Planning Commission to present the need for a new park system."

1. Amendment by addition (insertion)

PROPOSER: "I move to amend the motion by inserting the word 'three' before the word 'representatives.'"

PRESIDING OFFICER (*after hearing a second*): "It has been moved and seconded to amend the motion by inserting the word 'three' before the word 'representatives.' The motion, *if amended*, would read, 'that this organization send *three* representatives to the Council and to the Planning Commission to present the need for a new park system.' Is there any discussion on the amendment?... Those in favor of the amendment say 'Aye.'...Those opposed, 'No.'...The amendment is carried. Is there any discussion on the motion as amended?"

2. Amendment by deletion (striking out)

PROPOSER: "I move to amend the motion by striking out the words 'and to the Planning Commission.'"

PRESIDING OFFICER (*after hearing a second*): "It has been moved and seconded to amend the motion by striking out the words 'and to the Planning Commission.' The motion, *if amended*, would read 'that this organization send representatives to the Council to present the need for a new park system.'"

3. Amendment by striking out and inserting

PROPOSER: "I move to amend the motion by striking out the word 'representatives' and inserting in its place the words 'its executive committee.'"

PRESIDING OFFICER (*after hearing a second*): "It has been moved and seconded to amend the motion by striking out the word 'representatives' and inserting in its place the words 'its executive committee.' The motion, *if amended*, would read 'that this organization send its executive committee to the Council and to the Planning Commission to present the need for a new park system.'"

4. Amendment by substitution

PROPOSER: "I move to amend the motion by substituting for it the following motion: "I move that our organization hold a conference with the City Manager to determine how we may cooperate in securing a new municipal park system.'"

PRESIDING OFFICER (*after hearing a second*): "It has been moved and seconded to amend the motion that this organization send representatives to the Council and the Planning Commission to present 'the need for a new park system' by substituting for it a new motion 'that our organization hold a conference with the City Manager to determine how we may cooperate in securing a new park system.'"

What Motions May Be Amended?

The only motions that may be amended without restriction are the main motion and the motion to amend.

Four motions are open to restricted amendment. The motions to postpone definitely, to limit debate, and to recess may be amended as to time. The motion to refer to a committee may be amended as to such details as name, number of members, method of selection of the committee, or instructions to it, such as the time the motion is to be reported back to the assembly.

Amendments Must Be Germane

The most important principle concerning amendments is that they must be germane, that is, they must be relevant to, and have direct bearing on, the subject of the pending motion that the amendment seeks to change. For example, a motion "that the association pay expenses for its two delegates to the June 4 convention in Chicago" could be amended by adding the words, "not to exceed $500 each," because this amendment relates closely to the idea of the motion, which is to pay convention expenses.

If, however, an amendment is proposed to add the words "and that we raise the salary of the Executive Secretary," the amendment would not be germane to the subject of the motion. The presiding officer should immediately rule this amendment out of order, stating: "The amendment is out of order because it is not germane to the pending motion."

An amendment that would change one type of motion into another type of motion is never in order. For example, if a member moves "that the pending question be referred to the Membership Committee," it would be out of order for someone to move "that the motion be amended by striking out the words 'referred to the Membership Committee' and inserting in their place the words, 'postponed until the next meeting.'" This would change the motion from a motion to refer to a motion to postpone definitely, which has a different order of precedence. It is therefore out of order. However, instead of moving to *amend* the motion to refer, the member could move to postpone definitely, since that motion outranks the motion to refer. (This also would be simpler than going through the amendment process.)

Amendments May Be Hostile

An amendment may be hostile. That is, it may be opposed to the actual intent of the original motion. It may even nullify or change completely the effect of the motion. For example, the motion "that we condemn the action of the Committee on Labor in reopening hearings on the Wage Bill" might be amended by striking out the word "condemn" and inserting the word "endorse." Thus, the intent of the original motion would be reversed by a hostile amendment. But this amendment would be germane to the subject of the motion, which is to express the organization's attitude toward the action of the committee, and therefore is in order.

An amendment that merely changes an affirmative statement of a motion to a negative statement of the same motion is not in order. For example, a motion "that we employ a caretaker" cannot be amended by inserting the words "do not" before the word "employ." Such an amendment only reverses the order of taking the affirmative and negative vote.

Limitations on Pending Amendments

Amendments are of two ranks. Those applied to the original motion are amendments of the first rank, or primary amendments, and they must relate directly to the motion to be amended. Amendments to a pending amendment are amendments of the second rank, or secondary amendments, and must relate directly to the pending amendment. Amendments of the third rank are out of order.

Only one amendment of each rank can be pending at one time. When an amendment to a motion is pending, another amendment of the same rank is not in order, but an amendment of the second rank—an amendment to the amendment—is in order.

After an amendment of either rank is adopted or defeated, another amendment of the same rank is in order. Several amendments and amendments to amendments may be offered in succession, provided that only one amendment of each rank is pending at one time.

If the motion "that this organization entertain the veterans of Cleveland Hospital next Friday evening" is pending, and someone moves to amend it by adding the words "at a dinner party at the Wayside Inn," this is an amendment to the motion or an amendment of the first rank. If, during discussion on this amendment, someone proposes that the amendment be amended by adding the words "in a private dining room" after the word "Inn," this is an amendment of the second rank or an amendment to the amendment, and is also in order. But if someone proposes an amendment to strike out the words "Cleveland Hospital" and insert the words "the veterans of all hospitals," this is not in order because it is an amendment to the original motion and therefore an amendment of the first rank; since one amendment of the first rank is pending, no other amendment of the same rank is in order until the pending amendment is disposed of.

A proposed amendment to the bylaws or to a motion already adopted is itself a main motion and is subject to amendments of both ranks.

Debate on Amendments

When an amendment to a motion is proposed, discussion is limited to that amendment until it is disposed of. When an amendment to the amendment is proposed, discussion is limited to it until it is disposed of.

Reference to the main motion is permissible only for the purpose of explaining the amendment or its effect. When opposing an amendment, it is in order to say that if the amendment is rejected, the speaker will propose another amendment, which may be stated briefly.

Any amendment to a debatable motion is debatable.

Amendment by Substitution of a New Motion

When the wording or effect of a motion as proposed is not satisfactory, it is sometimes better, instead of proposing several amendments, to reword the motion and propose it as an amendment by substitution. Such an amendment must be germane to the subject of the original motion, but it may differ completely from the original motion in wording, purpose, and effect. The amendment by substitution of a new or reworded motion follows the usual rules governing amendments, and is subject only to an amendment to the substitute amendment. (See *When Can a Motion Be Renewed?*, p. 28)

For example, suppose the pending motion is to authorize publication of a handbook for chapters of the organization, outlining policies and procedures. A member might say, "Madam President, I move to substitute for the pending motion the following: that a section in our monthly magazine be devoted to chapter policies and procedures."

The motion would be germane, since it concerns the same general subject, i.e., keeping the chapters informed on policies and procedures. As a substitute motion it is a primary amendment, and therefore is subject only to secondary amendments (in other words, an amendment to a substitute motion cannot be amended).

Filling Blanks

Motions or resolutions are sometimes proposed with blank spaces for names, dates, or numbers to be filled by allowing members to propose suggestions. When no more suggestions are offered, the presiding officer takes a vote on each in the order of their proposal. Each member can vote for or against each suggestion. The name, date, or number receiving the highest affirmative vote is inserted in the blank. After the blanks have been filled, a vote is taken on the motion as a whole.

Withdrawing and Accepting Amendments

The proposer of a motion or an amendment has the right to modify or withdraw the motion or amendment at any time before the presiding officer has stated it to the assembly for consideration. As soon as it has been stated to the assembly by the presiding officer, it belongs to the body, and the proposer of the amendment can withdraw it only by vote of the assembly or by general consent.

If another member proposes an amendment that the maker of the motion wishes to accept, the maker of the original motion may save time by saying, "Madam President, I accept the amendment." (The consent of the seconder is not necessary.) The presiding officer then asks if there is objection to this acceptance. If no objection is made, the chair states that the motion is amended by general consent. If anyone objects, the amendment must be voted on in the usual manner.

Adhering Amendments

When a main motion that has amendments pending is referred to a committee, postponed definitely, or postponed temporarily, all pending amendments adhere to it and go with it. When the main motion again comes before the assembly, the amendments still adhere and are also before the assembly for consideration.

Voting on Amendments

Amendments are voted on in the reverse order of their proposal. An amendment to an amendment is voted on first. The vote is then taken on the amendment to the motion and, finally, on the motion.

If a debatable motion, an amendment to it, and an amendment to the amendment are pending, the procedure for disposing of them is as follows:

1. Discussion is called for on the amendment to the amendment and when discussion is complete or debate is closed, a vote is taken on it.

2. Discussion is called for on the amendment, either as amended, if the amendment to the amendment carried, or as proposed, if it lost. When discussion of the amendment is complete or debate is closed, a vote is taken on it.

3. Discussion is called for on the motion, either as amended, if the amendment carried, or as originally proposed, if the amendment lost. When discussion on the motion is complete or debate is closed, a vote is taken on the motion. A vote adopting an amendment to a motion—even an amendment that substitutes an entirely new motion—does not adopt the motion, and a final vote on the adoption of the motion itself is required.

Vote Required on Amendments

An amendment to any pending motion or amendment requires only a majority vote, even though the motion requires a higher vote for adoption.

An amendment to the bylaws requires whatever vote the bylaws provide; but amendments to proposed bylaw amendments, or to a pending revision of the bylaws, require only a majority vote.

Amending Actions Already Taken

If a main motion has been passed previously, it may be amended by a new main motion providing for its change. Since this motion to amend an action previously taken is a main motion, it may have amendments and amendments to the amendments applied to it.

An amendment to bylaws or rules adopted previously is likewise a main motion, but it requires whatever notice or vote is provided for the adoption of bylaws or rules.

Effect of Adoption
of the Motion to Amend

To change the original motion as the amendment provides.

Rules Governing the Motion to Amend

1. Cannot interrupt a speaker

2. Requires a second

3. Is debatable, unless applied to an undebatable motion

4. Can be amended

5. Requires a majority vote, even though the motion to which it applies requires a higher vote

6. Takes precedence over the main motion

7. Applies to motions that may be stated in substantially different ways: the main motion, to amend, to refer to committee, to postpone definitely, to limit debate, and to recess

8. Can have applied to it the motions to close debate, to limit debate, and to withdraw

MOTION TO REFER TO COMMITTEE

Purpose

To transfer a motion that is pending before the assembly to a committee:

1. To investigate or study the proposal, make recommendations on it, and return it to the assembly,
or
2. To conserve the time of the assembly by delegating the duty of deciding the proposal, and sometimes of carrying out the decision, to a smaller group,
or
3. To ensure privacy in considering a delicate matter,
or
4. To provide a hearing on the proposal,
or
5. To defer a decision on the proposal until a more favorable time.

Form

PROPOSER: "I move to refer the motion to the standing Committee on Education (*or* 'to a special committee of three to be appointed by the president,' *or* 'to a committee consisting of Mr. A, Mrs. B, and Mr. C') with instructions to report at the next regular meeting."

PRESIDING OFFICER (*after hearing a second*): "It has been moved and seconded to refer the motion to the standing Committee on Education with instructions to report on it at the next regular meeting. Is there any brief discussion on the motion to refer the matter to committee?"

Provisions Included in the Motion to Refer

The motion may be put in the simple form, "I move to refer this motion to a committee," or it may include provisions such as the type of committee, the number of members and how they are to be selected, its chairman, or instructions to it. If these provisions are not specified in the motion, the presiding officer may put the motion to refer to vote, and if it is adopted may decide on the membership of the committee and give instructions to it. Or the chair may ask the assembly to determine the detailed provisions either before or after the motion to refer to committee is voted on. These provisions may be included in the motion to refer if the proposer of the motion accepts them. They may also be proposed as amendments to the motion to refer to a committee, or in a motion proposed after the motion to refer has passed.

If the pending motion is concerned with a subject that is within the scope of a particular standing or reference committee, the motion is ordinarily referred to this committee by general consent.

When the assembly has voted that a committee be appointed, without further provisions, the presiding officer may appoint and announce the committee members at once or may take a reasonable time to consider the appointments and announce them later.

Debate on the motion to refer or on amendments to it is restricted to brief discussion on the advisability of referring or to such details as the selection, membership, or duties of the committee or instructions to it. Similarly, amendment is restricted to these same details.

Instructions to a Committee

Instructions from the assembly or from the presiding officer may be given to a committee as a part of the motion to refer, or by a separate motion, or by oral directions from the presiding officer, or in a memorandum from the secretary. Additional instructions may be given to the committee at any time before its report is submitted. After the report is submitted, the motion or assignment may be re-referred to the committee with or without additional instructions.

An assembly that has referred a motion or a matter to a committee may vote at any time to withdraw it from the committee, refer it to another committee, or decide the question itself.

If no main motion is pending and a member moves to refer a subject, problem, or proposal to a committee, or moves to create a new committee or to give instructions to an existing committee, this motion is a main motion.

Effect of Adoption
of the Motion to Refer

To transfer the referred motion to the designated committee immediately with any pending amendments.

Rules Governing the Motion to Refer

1. Cannot interrupt a speaker

2. Requires a second

3. Debate restricted to brief discussion on the selection, membership, or duties of the committee, or instructions to it

4. Amendments restricted to such details as the selection, membership, or duties of the committee, or instructions to it

5. Requires a majority vote

6. Takes precedence over the motion to amend

7. Applies to main motions only

8. Can have applied to it the motions to close debate, to limit debate, and to withdraw

MOTION TO POSTPONE DEFINITELY
(To Postpone to a Certain Time)

Purpose

To put off consideration, or further consideration, of a pending main motion and to fix a definite time for its consideration.

Form

PROPOSER: "I move to postpone the motion until later in this meeting when we have finished the reading of the budget."

or

"I move to postpone the motion until the next meeting (or convention)."

or

"I move to postpone the motion and make it a general order for the September meeting."

or

"I move to postpone the motion to the convention next year and make it a special order for two o'clock at the second business meeting."

PRESIDING OFFICER *(after hearing a second)*: "It has been moved and seconded that the motion be postponed to the convention next year and made a special order for two o'clock at the second business meeting."

Differences in Postponing Temporarily and Definitely

The motion to postpone temporarily (also called the motion to lay on the table, or the motion to table) defers the pending main motion temporarily but specifies no time for its consideration and is not debatable. Its effect terminates at the end of the current meeting or convention, at which time the main motion dies if the assembly has not voted to resume consideration of it (or to "take it from the table").

The motion to postpone definitely defers consideration of the pending main motion, but also fixes a definite date or time for its consideration, and may make it a general or special order for a particular time. Debate on this motion is permitted, but is restricted to brief discussion of the time or reason for postponement.

Limitations on the Motion
to Postpone Definitely

A main motion cannot be postponed definitely:

1. To a meeting or convention that is not already scheduled; for example, to a special meeting that has not been called.

2. To any time that would be too late for the proposed motion to be effective, if adopted. For example, a motion "to prepare an exhibit for the Centennial Convention" cannot be postponed definitely to a meeting later than the Convention.

Postponing as a General or Special Order

Any main motion that is postponed definitely to a particular time becomes a *general order* for that time. When that time arrives, the presiding officer states the postponed motion to the assembly for consideration immediately unless another item of business is pending. If another item of business is pending, the chair states the general order to the assembly as soon as the pending item of business has been disposed of.

To postpone a main motion and designate it as a general order for a particular time requires a majority vote.

Instead of designating a postponed motion as a general order, the assembly may vote to make it a *special order*. This means that when the specified time arrives the matter must be taken up immediately, regardless of whether something else is pending at that time. Any motion which is interrupted by the special order is simply put aside until the special order is disposed of, at which point consideration of the interrupted motion is resumed.

Because a special order interrupts pending business, a two-thirds vote is required to postpone a main motion and make it a special order.

If the assembly does not want to take up consideration of a

special order at the prescribed time, it may order further post-ponement, but only with a two-thirds vote.

Types of Postponement

A main motion may be postponed definitely:

1. To a later time in the *same meeting or convention* as a general or special order.

2. To a *later meeting or convention* as a general or a special order or as an item of business to come up under unfinished business at the specified meeting or convention. If a motion is postponed definitely to a particular meeting or convention but not to a specified time, it comes up under unfinished business at the meeting to which it was postponed.

A main motion may be postponed definitely as a general or special order to a time that is not stated but that is dependent on some other item of business. For example, a main motion might be postponed definitely "until after the report of the treasurer."

Consideration of Postponed Motions

If a motion that was postponed definitely or set as a general or special order is not taken up at the meeting for which it was set, it comes up as unfinished business at the next meeting.

When a motion that has been postponed definitely is stated to the assembly for consideration, it may again be postponed definitely to a later time and day.

If no main motion is pending and a motion is proposed to postpone definitely a motion that is to come up later, the motion to postpone definitely is a main motion.

Effect of Adoption of the Motion to Postpone Definitely

To postpone the pending main motion and to fix a definite date or date and time for its consideration.

Rules Governing the Motion to Postpone Definitely

1. Cannot interrupt a speaker

2. Requires a second

3. Debate restricted to brief discussion on reasons for, or time of, postponement

4. Amendments restricted to time of postponement

5. Requires a majority vote

6. Takes precedence over to refer to a committee and to amend

7. Applies to main motions only

8. Can have applied to it the motions to amend, to close debate, to limit debate, and to withdraw

MOTION TO LIMIT OR EXTEND DEBATE

Purpose

To limit or extend the time that will be devoted to discussion of a pending motion or to modify or remove limitations already imposed on its discussion.

Form

PROPOSER: "I move to limit the time of each speaker on this question to three minutes."

or

"I move to limit debate on this question to a total time of two hours."

or

"I move that the time of the speaker be extended by twenty minutes."

PRESIDING OFFICER (*after hearing a second*): "It has been moved and seconded that the time of each speaker on this question be limited to three minutes. This motion can be debated or amended only in terms of the nature of the limitations....Is there discussion?... Those in favor of the motion, please rise....Be seated. Those opposed, please rise....Be seated. The vote is 208 to 61. Since there is a two-thirds affirmative vote, the motion is carried."

Types of Limitations on Debate

The motion to limit debate on a pending question or to modify limitations already set up usually relates to the number of speakers who may participate, the length of time allotted each speaker, the total time allotted for discussion of the motion, or some variation or combination of these limitations. The most common example of a motion extending limitations on debate is one that extends the time allowed a particular speaker.

If one form of the motion to limit or extend debate is pending before the assembly, another form that does not conflict with the first may be moved as an amendment; for example, if the motion "to limit each speaker to five minutes" is pending, an amendment may be proposed to add "and limit the number of speakers to three on each side."

How Limiting Debate Affects Pending Motions

A motion to limit or extend debate may be applied to all pending debatable motions, to some of them, or to only the immediately pending motion. To illustrate, if a main motion, an amendment, and an amendment to the amendment are pending and the proposer of the motion to limit debate does not specify the motion or motions to which the limit is to apply, only the immediately pending question—in this case the amendment to the amendment—is affected.

Termination of the Motion to Limit Debate

A motion limiting or extending debate is in force only during the meeting or convention at which it was adopted. If the main motion is postponed until another meeting, the motion limiting or extending debate is no longer effective.

If no main motion is pending and a motion is made to limit

or extend debate on a motion that is to come up later, this is a main motion.

Effect of Adoption of the Motion to Limit Debate

To limit discussion on a pending question or to extend or remove limitations already adopted.

Rules Governing the Motion to Limit Debate

1. Cannot interrupt a speaker

2. Requires a second

3. Debate restricted to type and time of limitations

4. Amendments restricted to limitations, extensions, or removal of limitations on debate

5. Requires a two-thirds vote because it limits freedom of debate or sets aside already adopted limitations on debate

6. Takes precedence over to postpone definitely, to refer to committee, and to amend

7. Applies to debatable motions only

8. Can have applied to it the motions to amend and to withdraw

MOTION TO CLOSE DEBATE
(To Move the Previous Question)

Purpose

To prevent or to stop discussion on the pending question or questions, to prevent the proposal of other subsidiary motions except to postpone temporarily, and to bring the pending question or questions to an immediate vote.

Form

PROPOSER: "I move to close debate on the motion."

or
"I move to close debate on all pending motions."
or
"I move to vote immediately."
or (the old form)
"I move the previous question."

PRESIDING OFFICER (*after hearing a second*): "It has been moved and seconded to close debate on the motion before the assembly. Those in favor of closing debate please rise.... Be seated. Those opposed, please rise.... Be seated. The vote is 251 to 33. Since there is a two-thirds affirmative vote, the motion to close debate is carried. We will now vote on the main motion."

Confusion Caused by Former Name

The purpose of the motion "I move the previous question," first introduced in Parliament in 1604, was to suppress the pending motion. In the United States the motion was changed to a motion to close debate and bring the pending question to an immediate vote. Except in some legislative bodies, the old English name and form, which are misleading, have been largely replaced by the term "close debate." The forms, "I move to vote immediately," or "I move we vote now," also are sometimes used, and should be handled as a motion to close debate.

The motion to close debate is more than just a motion to end discussion. Any further amendments to the main motion also are prevented if the motion carries, and subsidiary motions are prevented, except for the motion to postpone temporarily, which has higher precedence.

Proposal of the Motion to Close Debate

The motion to close debate is a powerful tool for expediting business. It may be proposed at any time after the motion to which it applies has been stated to the assembly. It cannot be combined with the motion to which it applies; for example, the motion "I move that we enlarge our assembly hall and that we close debate on this motion," is out of order.

If the motion to close debate is proposed as soon as a main motion has been stated to the assembly, its adoption prevents any discussion of the question.

How Closing Debate Affects
Pending Motions

If the motion to close debate is unqualified—"I move that we close debate," or "I move the previous question," for example— it applies to the immediately pending motion only.

If more than one motion is pending, the motion to close debate should specify the pending motions to which it applies. For example, suppose a main motion, an amendment, and an amendment to that amendment are all pending. If the proposer of the motion to close debate wishes it to apply to both the amendment and the secondary amendment, but not to the main motion, this qualification should be stated. If the motion is to apply to all pending motions, this should be stated. If the motion to close debate on all pending motions is adopted, an immediate vote must be taken on the amendment to the amendment, then on the amendment, and then on the main motion. The motion to close debate may be applied only to successive pending motions and must include the immediately pending motion.

Termination of the Motion
to Close Debate

The effect of the motion to close debate terminates with the meeting or convention at which it is adopted. For example, if, after the motion to close debate is carried, the assembly postpones the main motion temporarily but resumes consideration of it later at the same meeting or convention, the motion to close debate still applies. But if the assembly votes to postpone the main motion until the next meeting, the motion to close debate is no longer in effect when the question again comes before the assembly.

Two-thirds Vote Required

The motion to close debate is the most drastic of the motions that seek to control debate. Common parliamentary practice requires a two-thirds vote to terminate debate.

Question!

The correct way to bring a matter to an immediate vote is to obtain the floor and move to close debate. A common practice, however, is to call out "Question!" without obtaining the floor.

This is clearly out of order when it interrupts a speaker, or when others wish to speak. However, when there is a lull in the discussion it often is merely an informal way of moving to close debate, and at the discretion of the chair may be treated as such. The chair may proceed by general consent ("The question has been called for. Is there any objection to closing debate on the main motion?"), or may take a vote ("It has been moved that we close debate. Is there a second?")

Effect of Adoption of the Motion to Close Debate

To prevent or stop debate on the motion (or motions) to which it is applied and bring it (them) to an immediate vote.

Rules Governing the Motion to Close Debate

1. Cannot interrupt a speaker

2. Requires a second

3. Is not debatable

4. Cannot be amended

5. Requires a two-thirds vote because it prevents or cuts off debate

6. Takes precedence over all subsidiary motions except to postpone temporarily

7. Applies to debatable motions only

8. Can have no motion applied to it except the motion to withdraw

MOTION TO POSTPONE TEMPORARILY
(To Lay on the Table, or to Table)

Purpose

To set aside temporarily a pending main motion in such a way that, if the assembly wishes, the postponed motion can be taken up again for consideration at any time during the current meeting or convention by a motion to resume its consideration.

Form

PROPOSER: "I move that the main motion be postponed temporarily."

or

"I move to table the motion."

or (the old form)

"I move that the motion be laid on the table."

PRESIDING OFFICER *(after hearing a second)*: "It has been moved and seconded that the main motion be postponed temporarily. All those in favor say 'Aye.'...Opposed, 'No.'...The motion is postponed temporarily."

Reasons for Postponing Temporarily

Frequently an assembly wishes to put a pending main motion aside temporarily without discussing it or to defer further discussion and decision until later in the same meeting or convention. The usual reasons for postponing a motion temporarily are that some more urgent business has arisen or that some members want additional information or more time before voting on the motion. It is also used to sidetrack an unwelcome motion.

The motion to postpone temporarily applies only to main motions and not to communications or committee reports.

Time Limits on the Motion
to Postpone Temporarily

A motion to postpone temporarily sets aside the pending main motion for the current meeting or convention unless the assembly votes to resume its consideration. Its effect terminates with the current meeting or convention.

During the same meeting or convention, the assembly may resume consideration of the matter, which has been postponed temporarily, by a motion to resume consideration of the motion.

The motion that has been postponed temporarily cannot be brought up again as a new motion during the same meeting or convention, but may be brought up at any future meeting or convention.

A motion that is postponed temporarily is postponed to an undetermined time. A motion specifying a definite time is a motion to postpone definitely.

Adhering Motions Also Postponed

When a main motion is postponed temporarily, all pending amendments and other adhering motions are postponed with it. If it is again brought before the assembly, all adhering motions come with it and must be disposed of in regular order. If the motion to limit debate or to close debate has been passed before the main motion was postponed temporarily, these motions remain in effect when consideration is resumed.

Use of the Term "to Table"

The early name of the motion to postpone temporarily was "*lay on the table.*" (In American usage the phrase has been shortened, and the motion is now generally referred to as the motion "*to table.*") The term grew out of the legislative custom of literally laying a bill awaiting further consideration on the clerk's table.

The reference to "laying the motion on the table" or "tabling" is still widely used, but the more precise term, "postpone temporarily," is preferred when that is its purpose, because the term is self-explanatory.

Sometimes, however, the purpose of the motion is *not* merely to postpone temporarily, but to set the motion aside indefinitely—in effect, to "kill" it, since a motion that was tabled (or postponed temporarily) dies at the end of the current meeting or convention if no motion has been made to resume consideration (or take from the table).

This practice of killing a motion by tabling it is used frequently by Congress and by most voluntary organizations, although it is frowned upon in some of the older parliamentary manuals. The argument against it is that the motion, being undebatable, permits a bare majority to kill a proposal without full discussion, which violates the principle that debate can be ended only by a two-thirds vote. However, the motion is so convenient a means of ending discussion and setting a motion aside that it continues to be widely used for that purpose, despite efforts to discourage its use.

To prevent misuse of the motion, a two-thirds vote should be required when the motion to table is used to prevent discussion of a motion.[1] Thus, if a main motion is being hotly debated and someone says, "I move that we table the motion," the presiding officer should say, "It has been moved and seconded that the motion be tabled. Since this would cut off discussion, a two-thirds vote is required. All those in favor of tabling the motion please rise.... Be seated. Those opposed please rise.... There being two-thirds in favor, the motion is tabled. The next item of business is..."

It should be kept in mind that the motion to table or to postpone temporarily does not literally kill the motion immediately: by a majority vote at any time before the end of the meeting or convention the motion can be brought back for further consideration by a motion to take from the table, or to resume consideration.

Effect of Adoption of the Motion to Postpone Temporarily

To stop debate on the main motion and remove it, with amendments and adhering motions, from the consideration of the assembly during the current meeting or convention unless the postponed motion is brought back before the assembly by a motion to resume consideration or to take from the table.

Rules Governing the Motion to Postpone Temporarily

1. Cannot interrupt a speaker

2. Requires a second

3. Is not debatable

4. Cannot be amended

5. Requires a majority vote (two-thirds when used to suppress a motion without further debate)

6. Takes precedence over all other subsidiary motions

7. Applies to main motions only

8. Can have no motion applied to it except the motion to withdraw

Chapter 9

PRIVILEGED MOTIONS

QUESTION OF PRIVILEGE
Purpose

To enable a member to secure immediate decision and action by the presiding officer on a request that concerns the comfort, convenience, rights, or privileges of the assembly or of the member, or permission to present a motion of an urgent nature, even though other business is pending.

Form

1. Question of privilege of the assembly (request)

PROPOSER (*without waiting for recognition*): "Mr. President, I rise to a question of privilege of the assembly."

PRESIDING OFFICER (*without waiting for a second*): "State your question of privilege."

PROPOSER: "May we have the windows in the rear of the hall closed?"

PRESIDING OFFICER: "Your request is granted. Will the ushers please close the windows?"

2. Question of personal privilege (request)

PROPOSER (*without waiting for recognition*): "I rise to a question of personal privilege."

PRESIDING OFFICER (*without waiting for a second*): "State your question of privilege."

PROPOSER: "May I be excused from further attendance at this convention because I have just been handed a subpoena to appear in court immediately?"

PRESIDING OFFICER: "Your privilege is granted."

3. Motion of privilege

PROPOSER (*without waiting for recognition*): "I rise to a question of privilege to present a motion."

PRESIDING OFFICER: "State your motion."

PROPOSER: "As a motion of privilege, I move that the secretary be directed to have the office prepare enough copies of the proposed amendments to the bylaws so that every member may have one before the evening business meeting."

PRESIDING OFFICER (*after hearing a second*): "As a motion of privilege, it has been moved and seconded that the secretary be directed to have the office prepare enough copies of the proposed amendments to the bylaws so that every member have one before the evening business meeting."

Member's Right to Request Privilege

A member has the right to request decision and action by the presiding officer or by the assembly on urgent questions involving the immediate convenience, comfort, rights, or privileges of the assembly, or of another member, or of himself or herself. A question of privilege may be in the form of a request to be decided by the chair or a motion to be decided by the assembly. The presiding officer may decide that a particular motion is not a proper question of privilege and rule it out of order.

Interruption by a Question of Privilege

The importance or emergency nature of a question of privilege allows its proposer to interrupt a speaker. When interrupted by a question of privilege a speaker should relinquish the floor temporarily, sitting down until the matter is settled. The presiding officer must rule immediately on the question of privilege by granting or denying it. Any member may appeal from this decision.

If the presiding officer decides that the request is a proper question of privilege and of sufficient urgency, the privilege is granted and the request is carried out immediately. However, if the chair decides that it is a proper question of privilege but can wait, the chair explains that the privilege will be granted when the speaker who was interrupted has finished. If the chair decides that the question of privilege is not a proper request, it is denied. As soon as the question of privilege has been handled the speaker who was interrupted is again given the floor.

Privileges of the Assembly

Questions relating to a privilege of the assembly have to do with the rights, safety, integrity, comfort, or convenience of the whole assembly. They frequently are concerned with the heating, lighting, or ventilation of the hall, the seating of members, or the control of noise. A question of privilege relating to the assembly takes precedence over a question of privilege relating to a member.

Personal Privileges

Questions of personal privileges pertain to an individual member and usually relate to his or her rights, reputation, conduct, safety, or convenience as a member of the body.

Motions as Questions of Privilege

Sometimes when one main motion is pending it is necessary to propose another main motion to take care of an emergency. The emergency motion can interrupt only as a question of privilege. The presiding officer will usually grant the member the right to state an urgent motion. If, after hearing the motion, the presiding officer believes that it needs immediate decision, the question is stated to the assembly and opened for debate, thus setting aside the pending business. If the chair believes that the motion is not urgent or is not a question of privilege, it is ruled out of order until the pending business is disposed of.

For example, if during a convention an embarrassing discussion arises which should not be made public, the presiding officer might allow a member, as a motion of privilege, to move "that nonmembers be required to leave the room."

When a question of privilege is presented as a motion, it is a main motion which is given special privilege. It follows all the rules of a main motion except that it may interrupt and has the precedence of a question of privilege. If it is noncontroversial, as it often is, it will usually be handled by general consent.

Effect of Proposing a Question of Privilege

To secure appropriate action by the presiding officer on a request or by the assembly on a motion in order to meet an immediate need or emergency.

Rules Governing a Question of Privilege (Request)

1. Can interrupt a speaker if it requires immediate decision and action

2. Requires no second because it is a request

3. Is not debatable because it is decided by the presiding officer

4. Cannot be amended

5. Requires no vote

6. Takes precedence over all motions except to adjourn and to recess

7. Applies to no other motion

8. Can have no motion applied to it except the motion to withdraw

MOTION TO RECESS

Purpose

To permit an interlude in a meeting and to set a definite time for continuing the meeting.

Form

PROPOSER: "I move that we recess for five minutes"
or (in a convention)
"until tomorrow morning at 9:00 A.M."

PRESIDING OFFICER *(after hearing a second)*: "It has been moved and seconded that we recess for five minutes. Is there brief discussion?... Those in favor say 'Aye.'...Those opposed, 'No.'...The motion is carried. The meeting is recessed for five minutes."

Difference Between Recess and Adjourn

A motion to recess *suspends* the current meeting until a later time; the unqualified motion to adjourn *terminates* the meeting. When an assembly reconvenes following a recess, it resumes the meeting at the point where it was interrupted by the motion to recess. When an assembly reconvenes following an adjournment, it begins an entirely new meeting, starting with the first step in the regular order of business. The only exception to this procedure is when an assembly adjourns to a continued meeting. (See *Continued Meetings*, p. 102.) This type of adjournment is really a recess.

Conventions often transact business for several days, and the series of periods for the transaction of business are actually one meeting. A convention, therefore, may move to recess to the next period for transacting business and then adjourn at the end of the convention.

Limitations and Restrictions
on the Motion to Recess

The duration of a recess is usually brief, but there is no definite limitation on its length except that a recess cannot extend beyond the time set for the next regular or special meeting or, in a convention, beyond the time set for the next business meeting or for adjournment of the convention.

It is usually desirable to set a definite time for reconvening, rather than moving to recess "upon the call of the chair." This avoids the anxiety members feel about leaving the immediate vicinity for a few minutes and thereby missing the resumption of the meeting.

The motion to recess may be amended only as to the time or duration of the recess, and debate on it is restricted to the time, duration, or need of the recess.

As are all privileged motions, to recess is privileged only if it is proposed when a main motion is pending. If it is proposed when no main motion is pending, it is a main motion.

Effect of Adoption
of the Motion to Recess

To suspend the meeting until the time stated for reconvening.

Rules Governing the Motion to Recess

1. Cannot interrupt a speaker

2. Requires a second

3. Debate restricted to brief discussion on the time, duration, or need of recess

4. Amendments restricted to the time or duration of recess

5. Requires a majority vote

6. Takes precedence over all motions except to adjourn

7. Applies to no other motion

8. Can have applied to it the motions to amend and to withdraw

MOTION TO ADJOURN

Purpose

To terminate a meeting or convention.

Form

1. Unqualified form (privileged motion)

PROPOSER: "I move that we adjourn."
or
"I move that the Eighteenth Annual Convention of the National Association of Broadcasters now adjourn."

PRESIDING OFFICER (*after hearing a second*): "It has been moved and seconded that we adjourn. Those in favor say 'Aye.'... Those opposed, 'No.'...The motion is carried. The meeting is adjourned."

2. Qualified forms (main motions)

   a.   Adjourn to a later time

PROPOSER: "I move that we adjourn to resume this meeting next Friday at 8 P.M. in this room as a continued meeting."

   b.   Making adjournment conditional

PROPOSER: "I move that, if the Committee on Finance does not report before ten o'clock, we adjourn at that time."

   c.   Fixing time for future adjournment

PROPOSER: "I move that we adjourn in ten minutes"
or
"at 6:00 P.M."

Qualified and Unqualified Motions to Adjourn

There are two forms of the motion to adjourn—the qualified and the unqualified. The simple unqualified form of the motion to adjourn is a privileged motion. It is privileged only when a main motion is pending, and if it is stated as a simple, unqualified motion that would take effect immediately if carried. The unqualified motion to adjourn may be proposed at any time except that it cannot interrupt a speaker or the taking of a vote. If the vote is by ballot, however, the assembly may adjourn while the ballots are being counted.

All qualified motions to adjourn are main motions, and thus are subject to debate and amendment. Even the unqualified motion to adjourn, if it is proposed when no main motion is pending, is a main motion.

Completion of Business
Before Adjournment

When a motion to adjourn is made, it is the duty of the chair to see that no important business is overlooked before putting the motion to a vote. If the chair knows of any important matter that has not been considered but requires action before adjournment, it should be called to the attention of the assembly. If the chair fails to do this, any member may call attention to the oversight. For example, if delegates have not been selected for a convention that is to be held before the next meeting, it is important that this be done before adjournment.

When attention is called to some action required before adjournment, the chair usually asks the proposer of the motion to adjourn to withdraw the motion until the essential business has been completed. If the member refuses to do so, and if the assembly chooses to disregard the warning of the chair, it has the right to vote to adjourn.

Adjournment to a Later Time

When an assembly cannot consider all its important business in the time available for a meeting, it is desirable to continue the meeting at a later time. The motion to adjourn the meeting until a specific time is a qualified motion to adjourn and, therefore, a main motion. No exact form is required, but it must be clear that the meeting is to continue at a later date, and the time and place of the continued meeting must be specified. No additional notice of the continued meeting is required unless provided for in the bylaws.

The interval between the current meeting and the continued meeting is, in fact, a recess, and the continued meeting is actually a part of the original meeting. (See *Continued Meetings*, p. 102.)

Adjournment and Dissolution

The general rule is that an unqualified motion to adjourn is a privileged motion if made while a main motion is pending. There is one exception to this rule. If an unqualified motion to adjourn is made when there is no provision for a further meeting of the organization, the motion is, in fact, a motion to dissolve and is a main motion. The presiding officer should call the attention of the assembly to the fact that there is no provision for another meeting and that the assembly might, in effect, be dissolved by adoption of the motion to adjourn.

A final adjournment that has the effect of dissolving the assembly or closing a convention is termed *adjournment sine die*, or adjournment without day.

Voting on Adjournment

After the vote on the motion to adjourn, the meeting is not ended until the chair announces the vote and declares adjournment. The *decision* on whether to adjourn, however, is made by the assembly, not the presiding officer. The chair cannot arbitrarily declare adjournment except when there is no quorum present.

A formal vote need not be taken, however. The chair, sensing that it is time to adjourn, may ask, "Is there any further business to come before the meeting?" If, after a pause, there has been no response, the assembly has, in effect, voted by general consent to adjourn, and the presiding officer may simply say, "If not, hearing no objection, the meeting is adjourned."

Frequently there is confusion in phrasing motions to adjourn. The presiding officer should find out which type of adjournment the proposer of the motion intends and then rephrase the motion, if necessary, to make it clear. For example, a member may say, "I move that we adjourn until next Friday at three o'clock." If the next regular meeting is scheduled for that date and hour, the member is merely calling attention to the time of the next regular meeting. The presiding officer should restate the motion as "It has been moved and seconded that we adjourn." In announcing the result, the presiding officer may add, "We are now adjourning until our next regular meeting, which is at three o'clock on Friday, December third." It is good practice for the presiding officer, in declaring any meeting adjourned, to state the time and place of the next meeting.

If the motion to adjourn is qualified and is in order, the presiding officer should call attention to the fact that it is an adjournment to a continued meeting, makes adjournment conditional, or fixes the time for future adjournment, and that it therefore is a main motion, subject to discussion and amendment.

Adjournment at Previously Fixed Time

When a definite hour for adjournment has been fixed by the adoption of a program, by rule, or by a previous motion, it is the duty of the presiding officer, when the hour of adjournment arrives, to interrupt a speaker or the consideration of business and to state that the time fixed to adjourn has arrived. A member should then move to adjourn, to suspend the rule requiring adjournment, or to set another time for adjournment.

Business Interrupted by Adjournment

Business that is interrupted by adjournment is affected as follows:

1. Business that was interrupted by adjournment of a *meeting* comes up as the first item under unfinished business at the next meeting.

2. Business that was interrupted by the final adjournment of a *convention* is dropped unless a motion or report is postponed definitely to a later convention or a committee is instructed to continue its work and report at the next convention.

Effect of Adoption
of the Motion to Adjourn

Terminates a meeting or convention with the announcement of adjournment by the presiding officer.

Rules Governing the Motion to Adjourn

1. Cannot interrupt a speaker

2. Requires a second

3. Is not debatable

4. Cannot be amended

5. Requires a majority vote

6. Takes precedence over all other motions

7. Applies to no other motion

8. Can have no motion applied to it except the motion to withdraw

Chapter 10

INCIDENTAL MOTIONS

MOTION TO APPEAL

Purpose

To enable a member who believes that the presiding officer is mistaken or unfair in a ruling to have the assembly decide by vote whether the presiding officer's decision should be upheld or overruled.

Form

PROPOSER (*immediately after the presiding officer has announced the decision, and without waiting for recognition*): "I appeal from the decision of the chair."

PRESIDING OFFICER (*after hearing a second*): "The decision of the chair has been appealed from."

The presiding officer then states the reasons for the ruling, and the member may state the reasons for the appeal. After opportunity for discussion, the vote is taken, not on the appeal, but on sustaining or overruling the chair's decision. "Those in favor of sustaining the decision of the chair say 'Aye.'...Those opposed, 'No.'...The decision of the chair is sustained [or overruled]."

When an Appeal May Be Taken

An appeal is the motion by which an assembly may review a ruling or decision of its presiding officer. Any decision of the presiding officer involving judgment is subject to appeal. The chair's statement of a fact, such as announcing the result of a vote count, is not.

An appeal is permissible only immediately after the presiding officer's decision has been rendered. If any other business has intervened, an appeal is not in order. However, if another member has obtained the floor, that member may be interrupted by an appeal if it is made promptly.

Statement of the Question on Appeal

The presiding officer must always state the question in the form "Those in favor of sustaining the decision of the chair...." The question on the appeal must not be stated in a biased form. For example, if a motion has been ruled out of order the chair could explain that the reason is that it conflicts with the bylaws. But the chair could not state the question as "those in favor of sustaining the bylaws...."

Statement of the Reasons for Appeal

An appeal is debatable because it may involve questions of importance to the assembly. The presiding officer states the reasons for the ruling without leaving the chair.

If the presiding officer's explanation convinces the member who has appealed that the decision is correct, the member may withdraw the appeal. On the other hand, if the member's reasons for the appeal are convincing, the presiding officer may change the ruling, and the appeal is automatically dropped.

Vote on an Appeal

The presiding officer's decision is sustained on an appeal by a majority vote or by a tie vote. A tie vote sustains the decision of the presiding officer because a majority vote is necessary to over-rule the chair's decision.

If no main motion is pending, an appeal is a main motion.

Effect of the Motion to Appeal

If the decision of the presiding officer is sustained by an affirmative majority or by a tie vote, the decision becomes the decision of the assembly. If the decision fails to receive an affirmative majority or tie vote, it is overruled.

Rules Governing the Motion to Appeal

1. Can interrupt a speaker because it must be proposed immediately

2. Requires a second

3. Is debatable

4. Cannot be amended

5. Requires a majority vote in the negative to overrule the presiding officer's decision

6. Takes precedence as an incidental motion and must be decided immediately

7. Applies to rulings and decisions of the presiding officer

8. Can have applied to it the motions to close debate, to limit debate, and to withdraw

MOTION TO SUSPEND RULES

Purpose

To permit an assembly to take some action that otherwise would be prevented by a procedural rule or by a program already adopted.

Form

PROPOSER: "I move to suspend the rule requiring that the reports of standing committees be completed before the budget is considered so that we may consider the budget now."

PRESIDING OFFICER (*after hearing a second*): "It has been moved and seconded to suspend the rule that interferes with the consideration of the budget at this time. Those in favor, please rise....Be seated. Those opposed, please rise....Be seated. The vote is 'Yes' 92, 'No' 18. Since there is a two-thirds affirmative vote, the motion is carried, and the rule requiring that the reports of standing committees be completed before the budget is considered is suspended. We will proceed with the consideration of the budget."

Which Rules Can Be Suspended?

When an organization desires to accomplish a specific purpose or to take a specific action, and is prevented from doing so by some of its special rules of procedure or by an adopted program, it may vote to suspend the rules that interfere with the accomplishment of the particular action.

Which Rules Cannot Be Suspended?

Suspension of the rules is limited strictly to procedural rules. The suspension cannot deprive members of any fundamental right. For example, an assembly cannot suspend:

1. A rule stated in a statute or a charter

2. A basic rule of common parliamentary law such as rules governing notice, quorum, vote requirements, and voting methods

3. A rule in the bylaws unless the bylaws contain a provision permitting the suspension of certain bylaws governing the method or order of considering business.

Restrictions and Time Limits
on Suspension of Rules

The motion to suspend rules may be made when no motion is pending, or it may be made when a motion is pending if the suspension is for a purpose connected with that motion.

Rules may be suspended only for a specific purpose and for the limited time necessary to accomplish the proposed action. Any suspension for a longer period would be an amendment of the rules and not a suspension. For this reason the object of the suspension must be specified in the motion to suspend the rules, and only action that is specifically mentioned in the motion to suspend the rule can be taken under the suspension.

A suspended rule becomes effective again as soon as the purpose for which it was suspended has been accomplished. If no main motion is pending, a motion to suspend the rules on a motion that is to come up later is a main motion.

The "Gordian Knot" Motion

Sometimes the parliamentary situation in a meeting becomes so confused that neither the chair nor the members can figure out how to proceed. In such cases debate can become bitter and counterproductive, focusing on procedure rather than on substance. If the group has no parliamentarian, or if the parliamentarian is unable to suggest any other way out, the best solution may be to suspend the rules in order to get a fresh start. This version of suspension of the rules has been described as the "Gordian Knot" motion.

In such a case, a member might say, "Madam President, in view of the confusion about the parliamentary situation, I believe it would be best if we were to cancel out everything that has been done on this motion and start over again from the beginning, permitting the motion to be resubmitted in whatever form the maker wishes. I move that the rules be suspended to permit this."

Such a motion usually will be passed by general consent, because members on both sides of the question are likely to be equally frustrated, and welcome a way out. If an objection prevents general consent, however, a two-thirds vote can suspend procedural rules.

Theoretically such a motion should never be needed, but in actual practice even groups which include experienced parliamentarians occasionally become confused and need a way of untangling a parliamentary snarl. The motion to suspend the rules can serve this purpose.*

Effect of Adoption of the Motion to Suspend Rules

Enables an assembly to take a specific action which is otherwise invalid under its procedural rules.

Rules Governing the Motion to Suspend Rules

1. Cannot interrupt a speaker

2. Requires a second

3. Is not debatable

4. Cannot be amended

5. Requires a two-thirds vote

6. Takes precedence as an incidental motion and must be decided immediately

7. Applies to no other motion

8. Can have no motion applied to it except the motion to withdraw

---

*Another way of starting over is for the maker of the motion to request permission of the assembly to withdraw it, explaining that the purpose is to reintroduce it in a modified form which would be more easily handled.

POINT OF ORDER

Purpose

To call the attention of the assembly and of the presiding officer to a violation of the rules, an omission, a mistake, or an error in procedure, and to secure a ruling from the presiding officer on the question raised.

Form

MEMBER (*without waiting for recognition*): "I rise to a point of order."

or

"Point of order!"

PRESIDING OFFICER (*without a second*): "State your point of order."

MEMBER: "The motion just proposed is out of order because there is another main motion before the assembly."

PRESIDING OFFICER: "Your point of order is well taken. The last motion is out of order."

or

"Your point of order is not well taken. The assembly just referred the main motion to a committee; therefore, there is no other main motion pending. Will the member who was speaking please continue?"

How Points of Order Arise

Whenever a member violates a rule, whether intentionally or not, the presiding officer should call attention to the violation and either require the member to conform to the rule or declare the member's action out of order. The presiding officer is, in effect, raising a point of order.

If the presiding officer fails to enforce a rule, of the assembly or of parliamentary procedure, or does not notice an error made by a member, or if an error is made by the presiding officer, it is the right of any member to call attention to the violation by rising to a point of order.

Rising to a point of order is a request that the presiding officer give a ruling or decision on the point raised by the member.

When a Point of Order May Be Raised

A point of order must be raised immediately after the mistake, error, or omission occurs. It cannot be brought up later unless the error involves a violation of law, or of the bylaws, or the accuracy of the minutes.

Since it is important that a mistake be corrected immediately, a point of order may be raised at any time, even though a speaker has the floor. The member making a point of order may interrupt a speaker by saying, "I rise to a point of order." This lets the presiding officer know that the member is entitled to recognition, even though someone else may have the floor, or may be seeking the floor.

Ruling on Points of Order

As soon as a member has stated a point of order, the presiding officer must rule on it, declaring that the point is "well taken" or "not well taken." The chair may state the reasons for the decision, if desired.

If the presiding officer is in doubt as to the correct decision, the ruling may be delayed briefly. Meanwhile action on the matter affected by the point of order is deferred. When a point of order raises a complicated or important question and the presiding officer is uncertain of the matter, it may be referred to the assembly for decision: "The member has raised the point of order that the amendment just proposed is not germane to the motion. The chair is in doubt, and will refer it to the assembly for decision. The question is, 'Is this amendment [stating it] germane to the motion?' Is there any discussion?...Those who believe that the amendment is germane to the motion say 'Aye.'...

Those who believe that it is not say 'No.'...The decision is in the affirmative; the amendment therefore is in order."

When the presiding officer refers a point of order to the assembly for decision, discussion is not in order unless the presiding officer invites it. No appeal may be taken from a decision by the assembly on a point of order.

A member wishing to challenge a decision of the presiding officer on a point of order must appeal from the decision of the chair.

Effect of Request for Point of Order

Interrupts business until the presiding officer either rules that the point of order is well taken and orders the mistake or omission corrected or rules that the point of order is not well taken and resumes business at the point where it was interrupted.

Rules Governing Point of Order

1. Can interrupt a speaker because a mistake should be corrected immediately

2. Requires no second because it is a request

3. Is not debatable unless the presiding officer refers it to the assembly for discussion and decision

4. Cannot be amended

5. Requires no vote, because it is a request and is decided by the presiding officer

6. Takes precedence as an incidental motion and must be decided immediately

7. Applies to any mistake, violation, or omission

8. Can have no motion applied to it except the motion to withdraw

PARLIAMENTARY INQUIRY

Purpose

To enable a member (*a*) to ask the presiding officer a question relating to procedure in connection with the pending motion or with a motion the member may wish to bring before the assembly immediately, or for information on the meaning or effect of the pending question; or (*b*) to ask the speaker or the proposer of the motion a question about the pending motion.

Form

1. Parliamentary inquiry

MEMBER (*without waiting for recognition*): "I rise to a parliamentary inquiry."

or

"Parliamentary inquiry."

PRESIDING OFFICER (*without a second*): "State your inquiry."

MEMBER: "Is an amendment in order at this time?"

PRESIDING OFFICER: "It is."

2. Request for information

MEMBER (*without waiting for recognition*): "I rise to a parliamentary inquiry."

PRESIDING OFFICER (*without a second*): "State your inquiry."

MEMBER: "Has this proposed motion been approved by our National Board?"

PRESIDING OFFICER: "Yes, it has."

3. Permission to ask a question

MEMBER (*without waiting for recognition*): "I rise to a parliamentary inquiry."

PRESIDING OFFICER (*without a second*): "State your inquiry."

MEMBER: "May I ask the speaker a question?"

PRESIDING OFFICER: "Is the speaker willing to answer a question?"

SPEAKER: "Yes."

or

"I will answer questions later."

or

"I am not willing to be interrupted."

Right of Members to Inquire

Any member has the right to inquire at any time about procedures directly connected with the pending motion, or with a motion that the member may wish to bring before the assembly immediately, or about the meaning or effect of the pending motions. This right to question is exercised through a parliamentary inquiry, which is a request and not a true motion, and therefore does not require a second.

When an Inquiry Interrupts

A parliamentary inquiry may interrupt a speaker only if it requires an immediate answer. No member should interrupt a speaker with an inquiry if it can reasonably wait until the speaker has finished speaking. In order that the presiding officer may know that a member is rising to a parliamentary inquiry and has the right to the floor while presenting it, the member should state that he or she is rising to a parliamentary inquiry, instead of merely waiting for recognition.

Inquiry Addressed
to the Presiding Officer

A parliamentary inquiry is always addressed to the presiding officer and is answered by the presiding officer. The presiding officer may consult with the parliamentarian, if there is one, but normally does not ask the parliamentarian to respond directly to the questioner.

If a speaker is interrupted by a parliamentary inquiry and the presiding officer decides that the question does not require an immediate answer, the chair explains that the inquiry will be answered as soon as the speaker has finished, and the speaker should be directed to continue. The presiding officer should never allow a parliamentary inquiry to be used as a method of annoying a speaker who has the floor and should refuse recognition to any member who is using parliamentary inquiries to harass or delay.

The presiding officer should answer reasonable questions on parliamentary procedure that are pertinent to the pending business. It is not the chair's duty, however, to answer general questions on parliamentary law that are not related directly to business before the assembly.

Effect of Request for Parliamentary Inquiry

Interrupts business until the presiding officer answers the inquiry or request for information, gives permission to ask the speaker a question, or rules that the inquiry is out of order.

Effect of Interruption

A speaker may agree to be interrupted for questions, or may refuse to permit such interruptions. If speeches are being timed because of limitation on debate, the time taken by the questioner is not deducted from the speaker's time.

Inquiries should be addressed to the speaker in the third person, through the chair: "Can the speaker estimate how long it will take to complete the study?" rather than "How long will it take you to complete the study?"

Members should not interrupt with a question if the inquiry could reasonably wait until the speaker is finished. The chair may overlook a very brief interchange when a member interrupts without first obtaining recognition, but should step in the moment a member who does not have the floor begins arguing with the speaker, and should call the interrupter to order.

Interrupting a speaker for a question is not a right; it is a privilege which may be granted by the speaker. It should be exercised only to obtain information, not to engage in argument.

Rules Governing Parliamentary Inquiry

1. Can interrupt a speaker if it requires an immediate answer

2. Requires no second because it is a request

3. Is not debatable

4. Cannot be amended

5. Requires no vote because it is a request and is decided by the presiding officer

6. Takes precedence as an incidental motion and must be decided immediately

7. Applies to no other motion

8. Can have no motion applied to it except the motion to withdraw

REQUEST TO WITHDRAW A MOTION

Purpose

To enable a member who has proposed a motion to remove it from consideration by the assembly.

Form

1. *Before* the motion has been stated to the assembly by the presiding officer:

PROPOSER OF THE MOTION (*without waiting for recognition*): "I withdraw my motion."

PRESIDING OFFICER: "The motion is withdrawn."

2. *After* the motion has been stated to the assembly by the presiding officer:

PROPOSER OF THE MOTION (*without waiting for recognition*): "I wish to withdraw my motion."

PRESIDING OFFICER: "Mr. B asks to withdraw his motion. Is there any objection?...There being no objection, the motion is withdrawn."

or (if any member objects)

"Those in favor of allowing Mr. B to withdraw his motion say, 'Aye.'...Opposed, 'No.'...The motion is carried and Mr. B's motion is withdrawn."

Right of the Proposer to Withdraw a Motion

Any motion can be withdrawn. Before a motion has been stated by the presiding officer, its proposer may change it or withdraw it without the assembly's permission, and any member or the presiding officer may request that the maker withdraw it. Usually such a request is made because some more urgent business needs prior consideration, or because the motion was based on erroneous information. At this point the maker may either withdraw the motion or decline to do so.

Permission to Withdraw a Motion

After a motion has been stated to the assembly by the presiding officer, it becomes the property of that body, and the proposer may withdraw it only if no objection is raised. If a member objects, the proposer or some other member may move that the proposer "be allowed to withdraw the motion." This motion is undebatable, can have no other motions applied to it, and requires a majority vote.

The consent of the seconder is not necessary. A motion can be withdrawn if there is no objection, or with permission from the assembly, up to the moment the final vote on it is taken, even though other motions affecting it may be pending or debate has been limited or closed. When a motion is withdrawn, all motions adhering to it are also withdrawn.

Recording Withdrawn Motions

A motion that is withdrawn after it has been stated by the presiding officer is recorded in the minutes with a statement that it was withdrawn. No mention is made in the minutes of a motion that is withdrawn before it has been stated to the assembly by the presiding officer.

Effect of Request to Withdraw a Motion

To remove a motion that has been proposed from the consideration of the assembly.

Rules Governing Request to Withdraw a Motion

1. Can interrupt a speaker

2. Requires no second because it is a request

3. Is not debatable

4. Cannot be amended

5. Requires no vote because it is a request and is decided by the presiding officer

6. Takes precedence as an incidental motion and must be decided immediately

7. Applies to all motions

8. Can have no motion applied to it

REQUEST FOR DIVISION OF QUESTION

Purpose

To divide a motion that is composed of two or more independent parts into individual motions that may be considered and voted on separately.

Form

Assume that the following motion has been introduced: "I move that an educational foundation be established by this organization and that a library of technical books be created for the use of our members."

MEMBER: "I request that the motion be divided into two motions: (1) 'That an educational foundation be established by this organization,' and (2) 'That a library of technical books be created for the use of our members.'"

PRESIDING OFFICER (*without a second, if the motion contains more than one distinct and independent proposal*): "It is requested that the motion be divided into two separate motions. This will be done. The motion now before the assembly is 'that an educational foundation be established by this organization.' Is there any discussion?"

Motions That the Presiding Officer Can Divide

When a motion contains two or more separate and distinct propositions, any member has the right to request that it be divided into separate motions. If the presiding officer agrees that the motion contains more than one independent proposition, it is considered as two or more separate motions, since members may favor one part of the motion but be opposed to another. To be divisible on the request of a member, the motion must consist of two or more propositions, each of which is capable of standing alone as a reasonable motion that might have been offered independently, and each of which must be suitable for adoption even if the other motion, or motions, should be rejected.

For example, a motion "that the salary of the executive director be raised by $2,500 per year and that new furnishings be bought for the national headquarters office" is clearly divisible.

On the other hand, a motion "that this organization erect a headquarters building and rent the two top floors to suitable tenants" cannot be divided because if the motion to erect a headquarters building were defeated, it would be ridiculous to vote on a motion to rent the two top floors. A request to divide such a motion must be ruled out of order. Resolutions or committee recommendations may be divided in the same way.

Motions That the
Presiding Officer Cannot Divide

There are certain situations in which a presiding officer does not have the right to divide a question at the request of a member. In these circumstances a motion to divide may be presented. If there is any objection to division of the motion by general consent, a formal vote must be taken. A formal motion also is required to divide a question when it contains several propositions so worded that they cannot be divided without extensive rewriting. Such motions are often referred to a committee to be rewritten.

When Division
of Question May Be Proposed

A request to divide a question is most effective if it is proposed immediately after the introduction of the motion that it seeks to divide. However, since it is an incidental motion, it may be proposed at any time, even when a motion to close debate is pending.

Alternative Proposals
for Dividing a Question

A motion to divide should state clearly how the question is to be divided (unless it obviously could be divided only one way), and any member may propose a different division. Such proposed divisions are alternative proposals, not amendments, and should be voted on in the order in which they are proposed. The proposal receiving the largest vote is chosen.

Effect of Request
for Division of Question

To divide a motion containing two or more independent proposals and enable the assembly to vote on each proposal separately.

Rules Governing Request
for Division of Question

1. Cannot interrupt a speaker

2. Requires no second because it is a request

3. Is not debatable

4. Cannot be amended

5. Requires no vote because it is a request and is decided by the presiding officer

6. Takes precedence as an incidental motion and must be decided immediately

7. Applies to main motions only

8. Can have no motion applied to it except the motion to withdraw

REQUEST FOR DIVISION OF ASSEMBLY

Purpose

To verify an indecisive voice or hand vote by requiring the voters to rise and, if necessary, to be counted.

Form

MEMBER (*immediately after the vote has been taken or announced and without waiting for recognition*): "Division!"
or
"I call for a division of the assembly."
or
"I call for a standing vote."

PRESIDING OFFICER: "Division has been called for. Those in favor of the motion that (*stating motion just voted on*) please rise. The secretary will please count....Be seated. Opposed, please rise.... The vote is 'Yes,' 62, 'No,' 47. The motion is carried."

When Division May Be Requested

A call for division is a request that an indecisive vote which has been taken by voice or the raising of hands be verified by a rising vote and, if necessary to determine the result, that the vote be counted.

Any member, without waiting for recognition, may call for division as soon as a question has been put to a vote and even before the vote is announced. This right continues even after the vote has been announced and another speaker has claimed the floor, but the right must be exercised promptly.

Any member who feels a vote has not been correctly reported has the right to insist on verification, but a member cannot use this privilege to obstruct business by calling for division on an obviously decisive vote.

Verification of a Vote by the Presiding Officer

The responsibility of announcing a vote correctly rests on the presiding officer. When in doubt, the chair should take the initiative in calling for a rising vote.

Effect of Request for Division of Assembly

To require the presiding officer to take a rising vote on the motion just voted on and to count the votes if there is any doubt as to which side prevails.

Rules Governing Request for Division of Assembly

1. Can interrupt proceedings because it requires immediate decision

2. Requires no second because it is a request

3. Is not debatable

4. Cannot be amended

5. Requires no vote because it is a request and is decided by the presiding officer

6. Takes precedence as an incidental motion and must be decided immediately

7. Applies to indecisive voice or hand votes

8. Can have no motion applied to it

Chapter 11

NOTICE OF MEETINGS
AND PROPOSALS

Importance of Notice

All meetings and conventions and certain important proposals require notice to members. The courts will not uphold the decisions of a meeting if the notice requirements for the meeting, or for any action that requires notice, have not been complied with. If there is proof that notice is purposely or negligently withheld from any member, actions taken at that meeting are not valid. The only variation from this rule is that a vote of *all* of the members may waive the lack of proper notice. (See *Waiver of Notice*, p. 100.)

Notice Protects Members

Common parliamentary law provides for the full protection of every member by rigid enforcement of notice requirements before a meeting. It does not protect absentees who have had notice but who fail to attend or members who come late or leave early. A member who has been sent notice of a meeting, or of an action that requires notice, and does not attend, relinquishes the right of decision to those who are present. When proper notice has been given and a quorum is present, it cannot be contended that those members present are "not representative" or that the meeting is "not representative," since legally all members are equal.

Notice of Meetings

Notice of any meeting must state clearly the date, the time, and the place of the meeting and should be signed by the secretary. The time and place of a meeting cannot be changed after notice has been sent unless notice of the change is also sent. Notice of any meeting sent so late that a substantial percentage of the members cannot attend is not valid notice, even if all other requirements have been fulfilled.

When the quorum of an organization is small or consists of less than a majority of the members, it is wise to provide specifically in the bylaws for the time and place of meetings and to state explicitly the time and place in the notice of each meeting. This prevents more than one group of members from meeting and claiming to be the official meeting of the organization. The notice of a meeting should:

1. State the exact time of calling the meeting to order so specifically that two or more separate meetings could not be held at different times in conformity with the notice.

2. State the place of the meeting with such certainty that meetings could not be held in two separate places even in the same building.

Convention notices are often issued in the form of a call to the convention. The call must give notice of the time and place of the convention and usually includes the method of accrediting delegates, and directions for sending in resolutions, reports of officers and committees, and proposed amendments to the bylaws. The call is usually sent by letter or is printed in the organization's magazine. A call can be in the form of a notice, a greeting, or in any form that makes it clear when and where the convention will be held.

Annual meeting may refer either to the annual convention of an organization or to that meeting of a local organization which is held annually at the termination of the organizational year to elect or install officers and to hear reports. Annual meetings require notice to all members of the time and place of the meeting and of any special business to be transacted, such as election of officers.

Regular meetings require whatever notice is stated in the bylaws. Any regular meeting of an organization may transact any business not requiring special notice. If the officers responsible for giving notice know that a proposal of great importance, but which may not require special notice, will be brought up at a regular meeting, they should, as a matter of good faith, send out notice of the proposal.

Special meetings require notice of time and place of meetings and also notice of specific proposals to be considered and decided, and of subjects to be discussed. At the meeting the members may amend the proposals stated in the notice but cannot consider any business that is not stated or reasonably implied in the notice. For example, the purpose stated in the notice, "to employ a new office manager," reasonably implies that the removal of the present office manager is imminent. Under this statement of purpose, however, the meeting could not consider the employment of a consultant. (See *Special Meetings*, p. 102.)

Continued meetings (that is, meetings that are a resumption of meetings that were adjourned to a particular hour or date) do not require special notice unless this requirement is in the bylaws. If either a regular or a special meeting that has been properly called, and has a quorum present, votes to adjourn to a later time, this is sufficient notice to those present. However, good organizational practice requires that notice of the continued meeting be sent to all members.

Board and committee meetings require that members be sent whatever notice is specified by the rules.

Notice of Proposed Actions

No proposal that according to the law, charter, or provision of the bylaws requires notice can be considered at any meeting unless proper notice of the proposed action has been sent to every member. Amendments to the bylaws or charter, sale of property, large and unusual expenditures, election of officers, and other items of similar importance require whatever notice is specified by the bylaws or rules of the organization. The proposals to be voted on must be stated specifically.

When an action that required special notice has been taken, any motion having the effect of voiding or changing the original action requires the same notice. For example, if a motion to lease property belonging to an organization originally required notice for its adoption, a motion to cancel the lease requires the same notice.

Waiver of Notice

If there was a mistake in a notice or a failure to send notice to every member and yet every member is present at the meeting, and no one protests a lack of notice, the members waive notice by the fact of their attendance and their participation in the meeting. Members may also waive notice by signing a written waiver of notice before, during, or after the meeting.

Chapter 12

MEETINGS

Meetings and Conventions Defined

A *meeting* is an official assembly of the members of an organization or board for any length of time during which the members do not separate except for a recess. It covers the period from the time the group convenes until the time it adjourns.

Convention usually refers to a series of adjourned or recessed meetings that follow in close succession. It is regarded as a single meeting with intervening recess periods.

The term "session" has two distinct meanings. It may refer to a single meeting, such as "a morning session," or it may refer to a series of meetings, such as "a session of Congress." Because of this confusion, the term "session" is not used in this book.

Regular Meetings

Most organizations have fixed times stated in their bylaws for holding meetings. Meetings held in accordance with these provisions are regular meetings. Since members are presumed to be familiar with the bylaws, no additional notice of regular meetings need be given unless the bylaws provide for further notice or unless notice of regular meetings is customary. The regular time and place for meetings that have been established by rule or custom cannot legally be changed without notice to all members.

At any regular meeting any business can be transacted that comes within the scope of the organization and does not require special notice.

No meeting may begin before the time stated in the notice or set by custom unless all members are present and consent.

Special Meetings

A special meeting is a meeting that is not regularly scheduled and is held to transact specified business only. Any special meeting of an organization or a board must be called in accordance with the bylaw provisions governing special meetings.

All members must be notified of a special meeting and the call or notice must state the items of business that will be considered and voted on. A copy of the call for the special meeting must be inserted in the minutes of the meeting. The order of business for a special meeting consists only of the proposals for consideration and decision and the subjects for discussion as stated in the call for the meeting.

The statement of business to be considered must be specific, and if action is to be taken at the meeting, this fact must be stated in the notice. If a notice states that one of the purposes of a special meeting is "to hear a report of the Refurnishing Committee," the report can be read, but no action can be taken on recommendations of the committee unless these are stated in the notice and it is clear that they are to be voted on at the meeting. Blanket statements describing business to be transacted, such as "any other proper business," do not give valid notice.

Minutes are not read at the beginning of a special meeting. Minutes of the special meeting are read and approved at the next regular meeting.

Provisions in the bylaws for special meetings of the whole membership of a large state, national, or international organization are unnecessary and unrealistic. The governing board should be empowered to handle emergencies.

Continued Meetings

When members wish to continue a regular or a special meeting at a later time, a motion to adjourn the meeting and to continue it at a definite later time makes the second meeting a *continued* meeting, which is legally a continuation of the original meeting. In effect, the interval between the two is a recess, even though it may last for days or even weeks. A continued meeting is sometimes referred to as an "adjourned" meeting. Since that term can be used for opposite meanings—a meeting that has ended, or a meeting that has reconvened—its use is confusing, and it is recommended that the more definitive term be used.

An organization can do any business at a continued meeting that might have been done had no recess been taken. Limitations at the original meeting remain in force at a continued meeting. A special meeting which has been continued can transact only such business as could have been transacted at the original special meeting.

Instead of following the order of business for a regular meeting, the continued meeting is called to order and the presence of a quorum is recorded in the minutes. Then, if some question was pending when the meeting adjourned, the secretary reads that portion of the minutes which concerns the pending question, and the meeting then continues from the point at which it was adjourned. Any business pending at the time the original meeting adjourned is still pending when the meeting is called to order.

Special notice is not required for a continued meeting, because it is legally a resumption of the original meeting, but it is good practice to notify all members of continued meetings.

Continued meetings may themselves be adjourned to later continued meetings. No continued meeting may be set for the same time as, or a time later than, the next regular meeting.

Failure to Call Meetings

If the officers or directors who are responsible for calling a *regular* meeting, such as a monthly or annual meeting of an organization or of a board of directors, fail to perform their duty and do not call it, a group of members or even one member may demand that the officers call the meeting. Such a demand is strengthened if an election or some important matter has been set for that meeting. If the officers or directors fail to call a meeting after a demand is made, statutes often provide that a group of members or a single member after a reasonable time may call the meeting and designate the time and the usual place. When a quorum is present, the meeting may proceed.

The bylaws of some organizations provide that a *special* meeting must be called when a petition from a specified percentage of the members is presented to the president.

Chapter 13

QUORUM

Necessity for a Quorum

A *quorum* is the number or proportion of the members of an organization that must be present at a meeting in order to transact business legally. If there is any question as to whether a quorum is present at the time set for a meeting, the presiding officer should not call the meeting to order but should determine the presence or absence of a quorum by counting the members present. *Until a quorum is present there can be no meeting.*

Quorum Requirements

The bylaws of an organization should state the number or proportion of members that constitutes the quorum. In the absence of such a provision, parliamentary law fixes the quorum at a majority of the members.[1] This quorum requirement is often too high, and most groups have a more realistic provision. The number required for a quorum should be small enough to ensure that a quorum will usually be present but large enough to protect the organization against decisions being made by a small minority of the members.

In organizations with a fluctuating membership it is wise to select a *proportion* of the membership as a quorum so the quorum will vary as the membership varies. Many organizations provide, for example, that one-eighth or one-tenth of the members constitutes a quorum. When a fixed number is required for a quorum, a reduction or increase in the number of members of the organization does not alter the number constituting a quorum.

In conventions where the business of the organization is

transacted by delegates who are expected to be present at all business meetings, the required quorum should be higher—for example, a majority of the delegates registered at the convention.

A mass meeting or an organization without a definite membership counts the members present, no matter what their number, as a quorum. A committee or board requires a majority of its members for a quorum.

Computing a Quorum

A quorum always refers to the number of members *present* and not to the number *voting*. If a quorum is present, a vote is valid even though fewer than the quorum vote.

In computing a quorum, only members in good standing are counted. The meaning of the phrase "in good standing" varies with different organizations according to their bylaws. However, a member in good standing may be disqualified from voting on a particular question because of personal interest or benefit in it. In such a case that member could not be counted for the purpose of computing a quorum for a vote on that question. The presiding officer is counted in computing a quorum.

If a quorum is present, a majority of those voting, which is often a small proportion of the total membership, has the right to make decisions for the organization. Since this is true, rigid requirements for notifying all members of meetings should be observed so that all members will have an opportunity to attend and vote.

Raising a Question on Quorum

It is the duty of the presiding officer to declare the meeting adjourned at any time it is apparent that a quorum is not present. If the chair fails to do so, it becomes the duty of any member who doubts that a quorum is present at a particular time during a meeting to rise to a point of order and request that the members be counted. Or a member may ask the presiding officer whether a quorum is present. This question is in order at any time.

The presence of a quorum is determined by counting the members present or by calling the roll. The presence or absence of a quorum at any particular time can be established by entering the number present in the minutes. When a quorum is obviously present, the question of the presence of a quorum cannot be raised repeatedly for the purpose of delay.

Presumption of a Quorum

The question as to the presence of a quorum at the time of voting on a particular motion must be raised at the time the vote is taken, if it is to be raised at all. It cannot be raised later. Unless the minutes show that a quorum was not present at the time of voting on a motion, the law presumes that since the minutes show that a quorum was present when the meeting began, a quorum continued to be present until recess or adjournment. It is not permissible at some later time to question the validity of an action on the ground that there was not a quorum present at the time the vote was taken.

Chapter 14

ORDER OF BUSINESS

Usual Order of Business

An *order of business* is a blueprint for meetings. It lists the different divisions of business in the order in which each will be called for at business meetings. Its purpose is to provide a systematic plan for the orderly conduct of business.

If the bylaws do not include an order of business, parliamentary law has established the following pattern:

1. Call to order
2. Reading, correction, approval, or disposition of minutes of previous meetings
3. Reports of officers
4. Reports of boards and standing committees
5. Reports of special committees
6. Unfinished business
7. New business
8. Announcements
9. Adjournment

When there is a prayer, an opening ceremony, or a roll call, it should follow the call to order.

Some organizations also include in their order of business an informal period called "general good and welfare," or in some fraternal organizations, "good of the order." During this period, which comes just before adjournment, members may make suggestions or announcements but no motions may be proposed. Some organizations also include under this heading a program, such as a guest speaker or entertainment, although the more common practice is to adjourn the business meeting prior to the program or to activities of a social nature.

Flexibility in the Order of Business

The regular order of business should be followed, but should have reasonable flexibility. For example, if no standing committee is ready to report but a special committee is ready, the presiding officer might state, "The Committee on Membership is not ready to report until later in the meeting. Is there any objection to hearing at this time the report of the Special Committee on a New Bookkeeping System?" If there is objection, a vote must be taken to authorize the variation from the regular order of business.

The order of business for a special meeting consists only of the call to order, consideration of the items of business stated in the notice of the meeting, and adjournment.

The order of business of a convention should be prepared to fulfill the particular needs of the convention. When a program or schedule for a business meeting has been adopted by a convention and a time fixed for considering certain items of business, this schedule cannot be deviated from except by general consent or by majority vote. If an item that has been set for a particular time is postponed to a later time in the same meeting, the motion to postpone is sufficient notice to all delegates present.

Agenda

An *agenda* is a list of the specific items under each division of the order of business that the officers or board plan to present to a meeting.

The list under "unfinished business," for example, would include any item of business that was interrupted by the adjournment of the previous meeting or any motion that was postponed definitely to the current meeting.

An agenda is usually prepared by the president and the secretary and is sometimes mailed to the members. Unless the organization has a rule to the contrary, the use or even the adoption of an agenda does not preclude other items of business from being proposed, considered, and decided during the meeting. An agenda is flexible, and items may be changed or omitted by the presiding officer, or by general consent, or by a majority vote.

Consent Agenda

Organizations having a large number of routine matters to approve often save time by use of a *consent agenda,* also called a *consent calendar* or *unanimous consent agenda.* This is a portion of the printed agenda listing matters that are expected to be noncontroversial and on which there are likely to be no questions.

Before taking the vote, the chair allows time for the members to read the list to determine if it includes any matters on which they may have a question, or which they would like to discuss or oppose. Any member has a right to remove any item from the consent agenda, in which case it is transferred to the regular agenda so that it may be considered and voted on separately. The remaining items are then unanimously approved *en bloc* without discussion, saving the time that would be required for individual votes.

Call to Order

The presiding officer calls the meeting to order promptly at the scheduled time by rapping with the gavel and announcing: "The meeting will please come to order," or "The Eighty-third Annual Meeting of the House of Delegates of the American Dental Association is now convened."

Reading of Minutes

Unless there is a prayer, ceremony, or roll call, the first business is the reading, correction, and approval of the minutes of the previous meeting. The presiding officer directs the secretary to read the minutes. When the minutes have been read, the presiding officer inquires, "Are there any corrections to the minutes?" If there are no corrections, the presiding officer continues, "If not, the minutes are approved as read," or some member may move that the minutes be approved. When corrections are suggested and there is a difference of opinion on them, the presiding officer takes a vote on the corrections before the minutes are approved. After the corrections are settled, some member may move to approve the minutes as corrected, or the presiding officer may state, "If there is no objection, the minutes will be approved as corrected. Is there any objection?" If there is an objection, a vote must be taken on approving the minutes.

If minutes have been printed and sent to each member before the meeting, they usually are not read in the meeting or convention. The presiding officer must call for corrections, however, before the minutes may be approved.

To save time, some organizations have a standing committee on minutes which corrects the minutes and reports at regular intervals. Others have minutes examined by the executive committee. After such a committee has certified that the minutes are correct (or has corrected them), the body may approve them by general consent or by majority vote.

Minutes of an annual meeting or convention are approved by a standing or special committee, or by the board.

Postponement of Reading of Minutes

The reading of the minutes may be postponed to a definite time or to a subsequent meeting by general consent or by majority vote, although this generally is not advisable. If the reading of the minutes of several previous meetings has been postponed to the current meeting, the presiding officer directs the secretary to read all minutes that have not been corrected and approved.

"Dispensing" with Reading of Minutes

Often a motion is made to "dispense with the reading of the minutes." This phrase is confusing, because it is interpreted differently in different organizations. It sometimes is used to mean that the reading of the minutes shall be *postponed* to a later time, in which case it is less confusing to move "that the reading of the minutes be postponed" until the specified time. Sometimes it means that the minutes shall not be read aloud, but that the printed version which has been distributed should be approved. In this case it is preferable to move "that the minutes be approved as printed."

Sometimes the motion to "dispense with the reading of the minutes" is intended as a motion to *omit* the reading of the minutes, even though no printed draft has been submitted to the assembly, and to certify them as correct without anyone but the secretary knowing what they contain. *This procedure is out of order.* It must be remembered that until the minutes have been approved they are not official minutes; they are merely the secretary's understanding of what was done in the meeting, and do not constitute a legal record of what happened. Moreover, to omit both the reading and distribution of the minutes is unfair to members who missed the previous meeting, because it deprives them of a summary of actions taken.

When an organization habitually "dispenses with the reading of the minutes," it is often because the minutes are too detailed, and are therefore boring. In ordinary societies, it usually is best to limit minutes to what is *done,* rather than reporting also what is *said,* and to omit irrelevant matters, such as the names of persons who second motions. (If a motion was acted on, the presumption is that it must have been seconded. Even if it was not, the absence of a second does not invalidate the action taken by the assembly, so recording whether it was seconded serves no purpose.) If the nature of the organization requires the keeping of very detailed minutes, it usually is best to submit them to the members in printed form.

Reports of Officers

The presiding officer usually calls on the treasurer to give a brief report. This may consist simply of a verbal report of the cash on hand or of cash on hand and outstanding obligations; or it may include a summary of collections and expenditures since the previous meeting, with mention of any unusual items. The presiding officer inquires whether there are any questions on the report. If questions are asked, the treasurer answers them. The presiding officer then states that the report of the treasurer will be filed. No action by the assembly is required on such a report.

Some organizations at this point in the order of business also call for reports from the president, secretary, or other officers.

Reports of Committees

When there is a report of the board of directors or governing board, this report comes first. The presiding officer next calls on the chairman of each board or standing committee and then of each special committee to report. The reports of committees usually are filed but not voted on.

If an officer or committee also presents recommendations, these are considered and voted on either immediately after the report or under new business, as the organization chooses.

Unfinished Business

The presiding officer introduces this section of the order of business with the statement, "Unfinished business is now in order."

Unfinished business includes only two types of items:

1. Any motion or report that was being considered and was interrupted when the previous meeting adjourned

2. Any motion or report that was postponed definitely to the current meeting but not set as an order for a particular hour

The presiding officer presents an item of unfinished business to the assembly by stating, for example: "Discussion on the motion to send delegates to the International Conference at Antwerp was interrupted by adjournment at our last meeting. The secretary will please read this motion." After the motion is read the presiding officer continues: "Discussion is now in order on the motion as read by the secretary."

The fact that a subject has been discussed previously does not make it unfinished business. Items of business that were postponed temporarily or referred to a committee are not unfinished business.

New Business

The presiding officer opens new business by declaring, "New business is now in order."

New business includes any proposal that any member may wish to present to the assembly, except items of business that must be presented under other divisions of the order of business. The opportunity to present new proposals continues until the meeting is declared adjourned.

Announcements

A meeting is expedited by having a regular place in the order of business for announcements and requiring that they be made only at that time. Before making announcements the presiding officer often will call first for announcements from members.

Adjournment

When a motion to adjourn has been made, seconded, and carried, the presiding officer formally ends the meeting by declaring it adjourned. Or, after asking, "Is there any further business?" and getting no response, the chair assumes general consent, and says, "Hearing no objection, if there is no further business the meeting is adjourned." But (unless there is no quorum present) the chair cannot, without a formal vote, declare the meeting adjourned if any member wishes to bring up additional business. The decision on whether to adjourn is made by the members, not by the presiding officer.

Chapter 15

DEBATE

The Right of Debate

The purpose of deliberative bodies is to secure the mature judgment of the group on proposals submitted to it for decision. This purpose is best served by free interchange of thought through discussion and debate.

The right of every member to participate in the discussion of any matter of business that comes before the assembly is one of the fundamental principles of parliamentary law.

Debate is regulated by parliamentary rules in order to assure every member a reasonable and equal opportunity to be heard. A knowledge of the rules governing debate is essential to every member wishing to exercise that right.

Extent of Debate on Motions

Motions are classified into three groups according to the extent of debate that is permitted on them. These are:

1. Motions that are fully debatable

2. Motions that are debatable with restrictions

3. Motions that are not debatable

Motions that are *fully debatable* are those that may require unlimited discussion for their decision. These motions are: main motions, to rescind, to amend (unless applied to an undebatable motion), and to appeal.

There are five motions that are *debatable with restrictions:* to recess, to postpone definitely, to refer to a committee, to limit debate, and to reconsider. Debate on them is restricted to a brief time and to specific points.

All other motions are *not debatable* and must be put to a vote immediately. To permit debate on the motion to postpone temporarily or to close debate, for example, would defeat the purpose of the motion.

Obtaining the Floor for Debate

As soon as a debatable motion has been stated to the assembly by the presiding officer, any member has the right to discuss it after obtaining the floor. A member waits until no one has the floor, then rises, addresses the presiding officer, and waits for recognition. The floor is obtained in this manner whether the purpose is to present a motion or to participate in discussion.

A member who has been recognized is entitled to be heard so long as the rules of debate are observed.

Recognition of Members During Debate

Usually the first person who rises and asks for recognition when no member has the floor is entitled to recognition. When several members seek recognition at the same time, the following rules help the presiding officer to decide which member should be recognized first:

1. The person who has proposed a motion or the committee member who has presented a report should be allowed the first opportunity to explain the motion or report, and usually also is allowed to speak last on it.

2. A member who has not spoken has prior claim over one who has already discussed the question. Similarly, a member who seldom speaks should be given preference over one who claims the attention of the assembly frequently.

3. The presiding officer should alternate between proponents and opponents of a motion whenever possible. When there are opposing opinions, the presiding officer may inquire of a member seeking recognition which viewpoint the member will present. Thus the presiding officer is able to divide the opportunity to speak more equitably.

Speaking More Than Once

No member or small group of members should be permitted to monopolize the discussion on a question. If a member has already spoken and other members wish to speak, they should be recognized in preference to the member who has already spoken on that question. However, if no other members seek recognition, a member who has already spoken may be recognized again.

Sometimes a few members who are interested in and informed on the subject being discussed will speak several times on that particular question. This is permissible provided members who have not already spoken are not seeking recognition.

What Is Not Debate?

A brief comment or remark by the proposer of a motion before stating it is generally permissible. Similarly, a brief explanatory remark or a question is sometimes permitted on an undebatable motion. An inquiry, or a brief suggestion or explanation, is not debate.

When debate has been limited, and a member responds to a question which was asked through the presiding officer, the reply is not debate and the time is not subtracted from the time allotted to the speaker.

Before voting on a question every member is entitled to know precisely what the question is and what its effects will be and is entitled to ask for a reasonable explanation or to raise a parliamentary inquiry. A member has the right to have a question restated before voting or at any time when there is uncertainty about its meaning or wording.

Relevancy in Debate

All discussion must be relevant to the motion before the assembly. A member is given the floor only for the purpose of discussing the pending question; discussion which departs from the subject is out of order. Illustrations or stories may be used in discussing a point so long as they are relevant to the motion under discussion.

If a speaker departs from the subject, the presiding officer should interrupt and request that the speaker's remarks be limited to the pending question. If the chair fails to do this, any member may rise to a point of order and call the attention of the presiding officer to the speaker's digression. The presiding officer should then direct the speaker to limit discussion to the question before the assembly.

Discussion is always restricted so far as possible to the immediately pending motion. When a motion is under discussion and a motion of higher precedence is made, unless the new motion opens the main motion to debate, discussion is confined to the motion of higher precedence until it is decided.

Dilatory Tactics

Dilatory tactics—that is, delaying the proposal or the vote on a subject by making unnecessary motions, asking pointless questions, or talking around and not on the question—are always out of order. As soon as it is evident that a member or group of members is using dilatory tactics, the presiding officer should point out that such conduct is out of order. If members persist in dilatory tactics, the chair should refuse to recognize them or should rule them out of order.

Members' Conduct During Debate

Debate must be fundamentally impersonal. All discussion is addressed to the presiding officer and must never be directed to any individual.

A motion—its nature or consequences—may be attacked vigorously. But it is never permissible to attack the motives, character, or personality of a member either directly or by innuendo or implication. It is the duty of the presiding officer instantly to stop any member who engages in personal attacks or discusses the motives of another member or is discourteous in word or manner. If the presiding officer fails to interrupt, any member may rise to a point of order and call the attention of the presiding officer to the speaker's misconduct. It is the motion, not its proposer, that is the subject of debate. Meetings must discuss measures, not people.

Arguments and opinions should be stated as concisely as possible. A speech is made not for the pleasure of the speaker or for the entertainment of others, but to assist the assembly in arriving at a decision on the question under discussion.

A member is more likely to be effective in debate when demonstrating courtesy toward the presiding officer and other members. Anyone who uses improper language or acts in a disorderly manner should be called to order promptly by the presiding officer. When a point of order is raised concerning a speaker's conduct, the speaker must be seated until the point of order is decided by the presiding officer.

A member who fails or refuses to speak in an orderly and courteous manner may be denied the right to the floor and, if necessary, may be ejected from the meeting by order of the presiding officer or by a vote of the assembly.

Presiding Officer's Duties During Debate

The presiding officer has the responsibility of controlling and expediting debate. A member who has been assigned the floor has a right to the undivided attention of the assembly. It is the duty of the presiding officer to protect the speaker in this right by suppressing disorder, by eliminating whispering and walking about, and by preventing annoyance, heckling, or unnecessary interruption. The presiding officer should insist that every member be attentive to the business before the assembly. The assembly owes respectful attention to the presiding officer and to each speaker.

It is also the presiding officer's duty to keep the subject clearly before the members, to rule out any irrelevant discussion, and to restate the question whenever necessary.

If there are aspects of the question that are being overlooked, the presiding officer may ask questions which will stimulate discussion of those points. The chair should seek to draw out all facts that will contribute to a clear understanding of the motion and its effects.

Time Limits on Debate

Parliamentary law fixes no limit on the length of speeches during debate. Each organization has the right to fix limits in its bylaws or rules if the members wish to do so. Debate can ordinarily be kept within reasonable time limits by the presiding officer's insistence that all discussion be confined strictly to the subject.

If debate has been limited, time allocated to one member cannot be transferred to another member. In legislative bodies members may yield portions of debate time to other members, but this is not permitted in ordinary societies.

Cutting Off Debate

It is unwise to make a practice of cutting off or preventing debate on most debatable questions. This is true whether debate is cut off by recognized motions or by arbitrarily bringing questions to vote without adequate opportunity for discussion. Members cannot be expected to maintain interest in an organization if they are frequently denied the right to participate in its deliberations.

Bringing a Question to Vote

When it appears that all of the members who wish to speak have done so, the presiding officer inquires, "Is there any further discussion?" If there is not, the question is put to a vote.

Some of the older manuals recommended that the chair ask, "Are you ready for the question?" when it appears that discussion has ended. This query, however, is often confusing to those not familiar with parliamentary procedure: they are uncertain how to answer it. It often causes someone to call out "Question!," which is not a proper parliamentary motion (see *Question!*, p. 61). Simply inquiring whether there is any further discussion usually accomplishes the purpose more smoothly and is the form more commonly used today.

The presiding officer should never end discussion arbitrarily. It should be ended only by the assembly, whether by general consent (i.e., by silence when the chair asks for further discussion), by a vote on the motion to close debate, or by a previously adopted limitation on debate.

If the presiding officer starts to put the question to vote prematurely, this does not cut off the right of a member to speak. A member, if reasonably prompt in claiming the privilege, can assert the right to speak at any time before the taking of the vote is completed and the result is announced. Debate is finally and completely closed by the announcement of the vote.

Informal Consideration

There are times when it is desirable to have discussion of a problem *precede* the proposal of a motion concerning it so that some agreement may be reached on the type and wording of the motion that is needed. There are also times when it is wise to set aside the formal rules governing discussion and debate. Both of these objectives may be accomplished by a motion to consider a particular motion, subject, or problem informally. Informal consideration permits freedom in the length and number of speeches, allows possible amendments and motions to be discussed together, and gives broader latitude in debate.

If no motion is pending and a motion for informal consideration carries, it permits consideration of a subject or problem before a motion concerning it is presented.

If a motion is already being considered by the assembly, the motion to consider the pending motion informally is an incidental motion. If it carries, the pending motion is considered informally until the members decide to take a vote on it. This vote terminates the informal discussion.

Sometimes an assembly wishes to consider a problem that is not sufficiently understood or formulated for a member to propose a clear and adequate motion covering it. There may not be time to refer the problem to a committee. Informal discussion often brings understanding and agreement and makes evident how the motion should be worded. Rather than offer a poorly thought-out motion, which will consume time and effort to perfect by amendment, it is better to consider the problem informally and then formulate a good motion.

For example, a member might say, "We realize that some action must be taken to raise more funds for this organization. I move that we consider informally the problem of fund raising." If this motion carries, the presiding officer opens the problem to informal discussion. When the problem is clarified and there appears to be a solution or a consensus, a member should offer a motion embodying the idea. This motion automatically terminates the informal discussion, and the motion is considered and voted on under the regular rules of debate. If no agreement on the problem is reached, informal discussion may be terminated by a motion to end the informal discussion.

Informal consideration has all the advantages and none of the drawbacks of the old complicated procedures of a committee of the whole (see p. 222).

Chapter 16

VOTES REQUIRED
FOR VALID ACTIONS

Significance of a Majority Vote

The most fundamental rule governing voting is that at least a majority vote is required to take an action. A majority vote is the vote of more than half of the members voting, unless the term is otherwise qualified. Jefferson said, "Until a majority has spoken, nothing has changed." It is obvious that to permit fewer than a majority to decide for any group would subject the many to the rule of the few, and this would be contrary to the most basic democratic principle. Democratic peoples universally accept decision by majority vote.

If a majority agrees, that is an agreement by the body, since all members by the act of joining the organization have agreed that the majority should govern. (See *Relationship Between Member and Organization*, p. 210.)

As a general rule, fewer than a majority should not be authorized to decide anything, and more than a majority should not be required for most decisions. Yet sometimes organizations adopt a rule that permits a mere plurality—that is, one vote more than any other candidate receives—to elect an officer. Others go to the other extreme of requiring a high vote on certain proposals. Sometimes such policies may be justified, but they should be used with caution, since under either of these rules the minority, not the majority, controls.

Any requirements permitting decisions by *less* than a majority vote (for example, by plurality) or requiring *more* than a majority vote (for example, a two-thirds vote on a proposal) are not valid unless they are included in the law, the rules of parliamentary law, or the bylaws.

Requiring More Than a Majority Vote

Some parliamentary writers have mistakenly assumed that the higher the vote required to take an action, the greater the protection of the members. Instead, the opposite is true. Whenever a vote of more than a majority is required to take an action, control is taken from the majority and given to a minority. For example, when a two-thirds vote is required, the minority need be only one-third plus one member to defeat the proposal. Thus, a minority is permitted to overrule the will, not only of the majority, but of almost two-thirds of the members. If a two-thirds vote is required to pass a proposal and 65 members vote for the proposal and 35 members vote against it, the 35 members have won; the 65 have been defeated. This is minority, not majority, rule.

The higher the vote required, the smaller the minority to which control passes. The requirement of a unanimous vote means that one member can overrule the decision of all the other members and thus exercise what amounts to a power to veto the action of the body.

Recognition that decision by a majority vote is an integral and vital element of democracy was clearly stated by Thomas Jefferson in a letter to Baron von Humboldt in 1817:

> The first principle of republicanism is that the *lex majoris partis* is the fundamental law of every society of individuals of equal rights; to consider the will of the society enounced by the majority of a single vote, as sacred as if unanimous, is the first of all lessons in importance, yet the last which is thoroughly learnt. This law once disregarded, there is no other but that of force, which ends necessarily in military despotism.

One exception to the principle of requiring only a majority vote is when the vote restricts the right of full and free discussion, as with a motion to limit debate or to close debate. These motions require a two-thirds vote. Another exception is when the rights of absentees are involved. For example, most organizations stipulate in their bylaws that the bylaws can be amended only by a two-thirds vote (and in most cases advance notice also is required). Bylaws of some nonprofit corporations (and some state corporation codes) require a two-thirds vote to buy or sell real estate, or to mortgage property owned by the organization.

As a general rule, however, it is unwise to require more than a majority vote to commit the organization to a course of action, because of the power it gives to a minority to override the majority's wishes.

Requiring Less Than a Majority Vote

The effect of deciding proposals or electing candidates by less than a majority vote is similar to requiring a higher vote than a majority. It takes away the power of decision from the majority and gives it to a minority.

Electing a candidate or deciding an alternative proposal by plurality vote (more votes than any other candidate or alternative proposal) means that officers may be chosen by a minority and that they therefore do not have the support that is behind a candidate chosen by a majority. If there is a large number of candidates for an office, the candidate elected may be chosen by only a small fraction of the members of the organization. No candidate can be elected to office and no proposal can be decided except by a majority vote, unless the bylaws provide for a plurality vote.

Importance of Defining
the Vote Required

Every organization should state in its bylaws the vote required to elect candidates and also the vote required for important decisions. Whenever the basis on which a vote must be computed is not defined in the law or bylaws, there is confusion as to the vote that is required. A majority vote means a majority of what? A two-thirds vote means two-thirds of what? Even a unanimous vote has several meanings.

The term "majority vote" sometimes causes controversy when the basis for computing the majority is not stated, and hundreds of cases have wound up in the courts because of the resulting confusion. For this reason, whenever such terms as "majority," "two-thirds," "three-fourths," or "unanimous vote" are used in bylaws or in standing rules it is advisable to qualify them by stating the basis on which the vote is to be computed.

Different Meanings of Majority Vote

A majority vote, or any other vote, may be qualified or defined in many ways. For example, in an organization consisting of 200 memberships (limited to 200 members) which currently has 180 members in good standing, with a quorum requirement of one-eighth of all the members, which is 23, if there are 150 present at a meeting and only 20 vote, a majority vote would be variously computed as follows:

A majority of all the memberships	101
A majority of the members in good standing	91
A majority of the members present	76
A majority of a quorum	12
A majority of the legal votes cast	11

A *majority vote of all the memberships* is often required to take an action in organizations having a fixed number of memberships. When this rule is applied to a board of education of eight members, a majority is five. If there are two vacancies, reducing the actual number of members to six, the required vote is still five because a majority of the eight memberships of the board is necessary.

A *majority vote of all the members* means a vote of more than half of all the members both present and absent. Such a vote is often required in organizations where the members serve in a representative capacity, such as a house of delegates or an executive board.

A *majority vote of the members present* is sometimes required to take an action. Under this rule the failure of some members to vote does not reduce the number of affirmative votes required. If there are 150 members present, an affirmative vote of 76 is necessary to act, regardless of the number voting.

A *majority vote of the quorum,* or a majority of the number of members who are authorized to act for the organization, is the minimum number that some organizations permit to make a decision for all the members. This is the vote required in many corporate boards of directors. It means a majority of those voting, assuming a quorum is present, with the further stipulation that the affirmative vote must include a majority of the number required for a quorum. For example, suppose a board consists of nine members and the quorum is five. There are five members present at a meeting and two vote for a proposal, one votes against it, and two abstain from voting. With this requirement the motion would fail—even though it has a two-thirds vote of those "present and voting" at a legally constituted meeting—because passage of a motion requires at least three affirmative votes.

A *majority of the legal votes cast* is the requirement that most commonly approves a motion or elects a candidate. When the term "majority" is not defined and no other type of majority is specified, the law holds that a majority of the legal votes cast is required. This legal decision has been agreed on to resolve some of the confusion that resulted when the basis for counting a majority is not defined. Unless it is qualified in some way, a majority vote means a majority of the legal votes cast. Unless stated otherwise, this is the meaning of majority vote when used in this book.

The legal theory under which the decisions of an organization may be made by a majority of those voting is that all the members have the right to vote if they wish to exercise that right. The members who fail to vote are presumed to have waived the exercise of their right and to have consented to allow the will of the organization to be expressed by those voting. The members who do not vote cannot be presumed to favor either side.

It is possible for a majority to consist of only one vote. A member may propose a motion that is of little interest to other members and when the presiding officer calls for a vote, the proposer votes "aye" and no one votes "no." The question is carried because it received a majority of the legal votes cast. A single affirmative vote, when there are no other votes cast, has been held by the courts to carry a question because that vote is the majority of the legal votes cast.

Plurality Vote

A plurality vote means more votes than the number received by any other candidate or alternative proposition. Thus, it may be less than a majority when there are more than two choices. A plurality vote does not elect a candidate or carry an alternative measure except when the bylaws provide for decision by plurality vote. For example, the result of a vote might be:

Candidate A	23
Candidate B	22
Candidate C	21

The total number of votes is 66. The first candidate has a plurality, but no candidate has received a majority vote (34). If election to office is by plurality vote, Candidate A is elected. But if the election requires the usual majority vote, no candidate is elected, and another ballot must be taken.

While election by plurality is simpler and quicker, it usually is not advisable. In the above example, for instance, Candidate A might represent an extreme viewpoint, whereas Candidates B and C both represent a moderate viewpoint, and perhaps a majority of the members would consider either of them preferable to Candidate A. Nevertheless, with plurality voting, the wishes of the majority in such a case would be defeated. In subsequent votes, as would be necessary with a majority requirement, one of the moderate candidates probably would pick up enough votes from the other to win; or, as often happens, the weaker candidate might withdraw, recognizing a hopeless situation. In either case, the interests of the majority are served.

Unanimous Vote

A unanimous vote on a proposal is a vote in which all of the legal votes cast are on the same side, whether affirmative or negative.

A unanimous vote for a candidate for a particular office is a vote in which one candidate receives all the legal votes cast for that office.

The essence of a unanimous vote is that all of those who vote, vote on one side or for one candidate. A proposal is adopted unanimously if one vote is cast for it and no vote is cast against it, or is defeated unanimously if no vote is cast for it and one vote is cast against it.

If the term "unanimous vote" is qualified in some way, the qualification determines the meaning of that particular unanimous vote. For example, the unanimous vote of "all the members of the board" means that all the members of the board must be present and that all of them must vote on the same side of a proposal. A unanimous vote of all the "members present" means that all of the members who are present must vote and that all of them must vote on the same side of a proposal.

A requirement that an action be taken only by unanimous vote is an example of decision by a minority—in this case a minority of one—and is a violation of the democratic principle of decision by a majority. It gives the minority "an absolute, permanent, all-inclusive power of veto." Three centuries ago, in 1693, the court of the King's Bench ruled that "the major number must bind the lesser, or else differences could never be determined." The requirement of a unanimous vote is seldom necessary or wise.

Tie Vote

A tie vote on a *motion* means that the same number of members has voted in the affirmative as in the negative. Since a majority vote, or more than half of the legal votes cast, is required to pass a motion, an equal or tie vote means that the motion is lost because it has failed to receive a majority vote. A tie vote on a motion is not a deadlock vote that must be resolved; it is simply not a majority vote and the motion is lost.

A tie vote that constitutes a *deadlock* that must be resolved can occur only when two or more candidates, or two or more alternative propositions, are being voted on at the same time and two or more of them receive the same number of votes. Then no candidate has been elected or no proposal has been adopted. Such a tie vote results in a deadlock, and the vote must be retaken until the tie is resolved by voting or by some other method which the assembly may choose.

Vote of the Presiding Officer

No officer relinquishes the rights of membership by accepting office, except that the presiding officer of an assembly cannot propose motions or nominate candidates. The presiding officer does have the right to cast a vote—but in an assembly the chair customarily exercises that right only when the vote is by ballot or when one more vote could alter the outcome. This preserves the chair's aura of impartiality and objectivity. As is the case with any other member, the presiding officer cannot be required to cast a vote.

Tie votes. In case of a tie vote the chair may vote with either side, thereby establishing a majority, provided the chair has not already voted. Or the chair may choose to not vote, in which case, lacking a majority, the motion is lost.

If a motion is about to be carried by a single vote, the chair may choose to vote against it, thereby *creating* a tie, in which case, lacking a majority, the motion is lost.

Ballot voting. When vote is by ballot, the presiding officer (if a member of the organization) votes the same as anyone else. But in such cases if a tie results, the chair cannot break the tie by voting a second time unless the bylaws provide that this may be done in case of a deadlock tie vote.

Computation of a Two-thirds Vote

Sometimes when a two-thirds vote is required an awkward pause occurs in the proceedings while the presiding officer does the arithmetic necessary to determine whether a two-thirds vote has been achieved. A simple formula can make the mental computation easier: Double the negative vote. The resulting figure is the affirmative vote required for adoption.

For example, if the vote is 87 in favor and 44 opposed, the motion fails, because twice 44 is 88, and the affirmative vote is one short of that number.

Computing a Majority for Separate Questions

When more than one question is voted on at the same time, or on the same ballot, the votes cast on each question are counted separately. A majority of the legal votes cast on each particular question is required to approve that question.

In an election, when candidates for more than one office are voted on at the same time, a majority of the legal votes cast for each particular office is required to elect a candidate to that office.

Computing a Majority
When Electing a Group

Frequently candidates for several positions or offices of *equal* rank, such as members of a board, committee, or group of delegates, are voted on at the same time. When the offices are of equal rank and there is no differentiation between them, the majority vote required to elect is computed differently.

When several equal positions are voted on simultaneously, the majority vote is based on the total number of *legal ballots cast for the group* of equal offices. Even if some ballots contain a vote for only one nominee, these ballots are counted in determining a majority of the total *ballots* cast.

When several offices of equal rank are being voted on simultaneously and require a majority vote, there are two requirements for election. The nominee must:

1. Receive a majority vote based on the total number of *legal ballots* cast for all of the equal offices.

2. Receive a vote that is high enough to be within the number of offices to be filled.

A candidate who receives a majority vote but fails to rank high enough to place within the number of offices to be filled is not elected. Similarly, a candidate who ranks among the highest candidates but does not receive a majority vote is not elected. For example, if five board members are to be elected at the same time and there are seven nominees for these five positions, with 95 members voting, the vote might result as follows:

Nominee	Vote
A	80
B	79
C	75
D	75
E	69
F	52
G	43

Six members received the necessary majority vote (48), but only the top-ranking five are elected. The two nominees who tied for third and fourth place are both elected. Therefore, there is no necessity to break this tie vote. However, had there been a tie between the fifth and sixth places, it would have been necessary to vote again and break this tie to determine which nominee is elected.

If only three of the nominees had received a majority vote, only those three would be elected; it would then be necessary to take another vote to fill the two remaining vacancies. Unless the assembly adopts a motion to the contrary, all nominees except the three already elected remain candidates on the second ballot.

Voting Separately for Equal Positions

Some organizations favor differentiating between equal positions by numbering each position and nominating candidates separately for each position. For example, candidates A, B, and C might be nominated as candidates for Board Vacancy No. 1 and candidates D and E for Board Vacancy No. 2. In this case, a majority of the legal votes cast for each particular position would elect a candidate. This practice may result in the defeat of a popular candidate and the election of an unpopular one. In the example given, candidates A, B, and C might be much more popular than the other candidates, but two of them are sure to be defeated, while either candidate D or E, despite relative unpopularity, is sure to be elected.

Sometimes the reason for differentiating is that one of the terms is, for example, for two years and the other one is for one year. A common way of handling this situation is for the two candidates receiving the highest vote to be declared elected, with the allocation of terms to be determined by lot. If the method is not specified in the bylaws or in the standing rules, a motion clarifying the procedure should be made prior to the election.

When Members Cannot Vote

There are certain situations in which a member has no right to vote. As a general principle, a member having a direct personal or financial interest in a matter should not vote on it. (Stockholders are an exception to this principle.) For example, if a motion is made to award a contract to a member, the member cannot legally vote on it. (See *Conflicts of Interest,* p. 174.) The courts have recognized an exception to this rule when the organization is authorized to fix the compensation of its members; otherwise, it would be impossible to vote to fix the compensation.

A member may vote on a question involving the whole organization when others are equally affected by the vote, even though the member has a direct personal or financial interest. For example, every member has the right to vote on a motion that determines convention expenses to be paid to delegates by the organization.

When charges have been preferred against a member, that member cannot vote on the charges. However, if other members are also named in the charges, all members can vote on the charges. This rule prevents a small proportion of members from gaining control of an organization by filing charges against the majority of the members.

Chapter 17

METHODS OF VOTING

Voting Is a Fundamental Right

A member of any democratic body has the right to participate in electing officers and in deciding propositions. The right to a voice in determining the will of an assembly is the most fundamental right of a member. A vote is a formal expression of the will of the assembly.

While it is the right of each member to vote on every question, in ordinary assemblies the members cannot be compelled to vote.

The proposer of a motion has the same right as any other member to speak for or against the motion, or to vote for or against it, because the proposer's opinion may have changed during the course of discussion, or the motion itself may have been changed by amendment.

Voting in Meetings

When the method of voting on a motion or candidate is not prescribed in the bylaws, a method of voting may be proposed by any member and determined by majority vote of the assembly at any time before the vote on the motion or candidate is taken. The usual methods of voting in a meeting are:

1. Voice vote

2. Rising or raising hands

3. Roll call

4. Ballot

Voice Vote

Voting by voice is the most commonly used method of voting. The presiding officer determines the result of the vote by the volume of voices. When in doubt as to how the majority voted, the chair may call for the vote again, asking for a rising vote (a *division of the assembly*) or a show of hands.

Any member who believes that a vote is indecisive or that the presiding officer has not announced it correctly, may interrupt, if necessary, and call for a division of the assembly to verify the vote. This demand must be made promptly.

In taking a vote by any method, the presiding officer must always call for the affirmative vote first and announce it first.

The negative vote always must be called for, even if the affirmative vote appears to be overwhelming or unanimous. The only exception is a courtesy vote, such as a vote thanking a speaker for participating.

Rising Vote

A rising vote (also called a standing vote) may be used by the presiding officer to verify an indecisive vote or in response to a call from a member for a division of the assembly. The vote on a motion requiring a definite number or proportion of votes, such as two-thirds, is usually taken initially by rising so that a count may be made.

When the rising vote is close, the members should be counted; they *must* be counted if a count is demanded by a member and if there is any doubt as to the result of the vote. The presiding officer usually asks the secretary to count the vote. In a convention or a large meeting the chair appoints several tellers to assist the secretary. Each teller counts a particular section of voters and reports to the secretary, who announces the number of votes for and against the motion. The presiding officer then repeats the totals and announces the result: "The vote is 148 affirmative, 150 negative. The motion is lost."

In very large assemblies one way of ensuring accuracy in counting a rising vote is a *serpentine* count. Members in favor stand, then beginning with the first row each person counts off and sits down, with the count running back and forth along the rows in serpentine fashion. When all are seated the same is done with the negative vote. This minimizes the risk of any error in the count.

When visitors or others who are not entitled to vote are seated with members, votes should be taken only by rising, raising hands, or by roll call.

Roll Call Vote

A recorded vote is often advantageous when members vote as representatives of others, for example, delegates, proxies, or members of governmental boards or commissions. A roll call vote is sometimes termed "voting by yeas and nays." A vote by roll call may be required by the bylaws or may be decided upon by the assembly following a motion from a member. A majority vote is required to order a roll call. The presiding officer states the question on a roll call as follows: "The motion is... Those in favor of the motion will vote 'Aye' [or 'Yea'] as their names are called; those opposed will vote 'No' [or 'Nay']. The secretary will call the roll."

The names are called in alphabetical order, or in the numerical order of districts, or in some other appropriate order. The name of the presiding officer is usually called last. A member who does not wish to vote may remain silent or answer "present" or "abstaining." The secretary should always have lists of names ready for use in calling the roll, and should repeat each member's vote to ensure that it is recorded correctly. The original roll call record is inserted in the minutes.

Ballot Vote

Voting by ballot is the only method that enables members to express their decisions without revealing their opinions or preferences. (The use of a voting machine or any other method in which the person expressing a choice cannot be identified with the choice expressed is considered a form of voting by ballot.) Secrecy is implicit in a ballot vote, and an election requiring a ballot vote may be invalidated by the courts if it is shown that by any means (such as numbering of ballots in a way that would identify the voter) it would be possible to determine how an individual voted.

A ballot vote is usually required in elections and frequently in voting on important proposals. If a ballot vote on a particular motion is not required by the bylaws, it may be ordered by a motion to vote by ballot on the particular question. If a vote by ballot is required by the bylaws, a motion to dispense with the ballot vote, or to suspend the provision requiring such a vote, is not in order unless this procedure is provided for in the bylaws. (See *Casting of Ballot by the Secretary*, p. 149.)

The presiding officer should give careful instructions as to how the members should prepare their ballots and should ask before the voting begins whether anyone is without a ballot.

Voting by General Consent

Routine or noncontroversial questions are often decided by *general consent*, without taking a formal vote. When members are in agreement, this method (often called *"unanimous consent"**) saves time and expedites business.

For example, if a member moves "that the calling of the roll be dispensed with," the presiding officer may respond, "It has been moved and seconded that the calling of the roll be dispensed with. Is there any objection?" If any member says, "I object," a vote must be taken on the motion.

The presiding officer may propose action by general consent without any motion, or may proceed by assuming general consent. For example, if a member asks to make an announcement at an unusual time, the presiding officer may say, "If there is no objection, the member will be allowed to make an announcement now." Even when the presiding officer has announced that an action has been taken by general consent, if any member immediately objects, the question must be stated and voted on.

Voting by Mail

In organizations whose members are scattered over a wide area or who work during different hours, provision is sometimes made

---

* The term "unanimous consent," which means that unanimity is assumed because no one objects, is sometimes confused with "unanimous vote," which means that a vote was actually taken, and everyone voted the same way. To avoid confusion the term "general consent" is preferred.

for members to vote on important questions by mail. Voting by mail cannot be used unless it is authorized in the bylaws.

Voting by mail has certain disadvantages. When voting by mail, the members do not have the opportunity to discuss or listen to debate on proposals or to amend them. In elections there is no opportunity to nominate candidates from the floor.

Voting by mail by some members who cannot attend a meeting and voting at a meeting or convention by those who attend cannot be combined successfully. Since proposals and amendments to bylaws can be discussed and amended at a meeting or convention, those voting by mail and those voting at a convention might each be voting on quite different proposals or amendments. Similarly, when candidates are being elected, those voting by mail would have no chance to nominate additional candidates from the floor or to consider candidates nominated from the floor.

An organization should choose between voting on proposals or amendments to the bylaws by mail and the right to discuss, amend, and vote on them at a meeting or convention. It should similarly choose between voting for candidates by mail and the right to nominate additional candidates from the floor.

Any method of voting by mail may be followed so long as it ensures the voters full understanding of the issues to be decided. Unless the bylaws provide for a particular plan, a ballot containing proposed measures or amendments or a list of candidates is mailed to each member by the secretary together with directions from the elections committee for voting. Some organizations include with the ballot information concerning qualifications of candidates and arguments for and against proposals to be voted on.

The ballot must be marked and returned to the secretary within a specified time. The usual way to preserve secrecy in a mail vote is to provide each member with a blank envelope which has no mark of identification on it. The marked ballot is placed in this envelope, which is then sealed. It in turn is enclosed in another envelope which the member signs, so that the member's name may be checked against the list of members eligible to vote. The blank inner envelope is delivered, still sealed, to the tellers or election committee.

Voting by Proxy

Voting by proxy means that a particular member or person is authorized to cast the vote of an absent member in a meeting or convention. The term "proxy" may mean either the statement authorizing a member to cast the vote of the member signing it or the member who casts the vote. The proxy voter may cast one vote for each proxy held.

In profit corporations, where membership is based on the ownership of shares of stock and voting rights are unequal, voting by proxy is the approved method of deciding proposals and electing officers.

In nonprofit corporations or organizations, voting by proxy is legal in most states only if it is authorized by statute and provided for in the charter and bylaws of the organization. Directors or board members cannot vote by proxy in their meetings, since this would mean the delegation of a discretionary legislative duty which they cannot delegate.

A proxy may be in almost any form as long as its meaning is clear. It may be limited to one meeting, or motion, or issue, or person, or time, or it may be unlimited. All proxies, however, must conform strictly to the provisions of the statutes and charters, and to the bylaws of the organization. The use of proxies in organizations in which all members have an equal vote is ill advised and is never permissible unless specifically authorized by the bylaws, charters, or statutes.

Changing a Vote

When a vote is taken by a show of hands, by rising, or by roll call, members may change their votes up to the time that the result of the vote is finally announced. After a vote by roll call has been announced, a member may change a vote only by proof that an error was made in recording it. When voting is by ballot, a member may not change the ballot after it has been placed in the ballot box.

Announcing the Result of a Vote

It is the duty of the presiding officer to announce the result of the vote according to the facts. However, an incorrect or untrue announcement of the vote cannot make the vote as cast by the majority illegal. In case of a disputed vote, the courts will examine the facts to determine whether the vote as announced is correct.

All Votes Binding During a Meeting

A few organizations follow the improper practice of taking an informal test, or straw vote in meetings, which they interpret to be a vote that is not binding. Such a vote is sometimes used to influence members to reach a consensus. A unity of opinion, if it is reached without coercion, is desirable; but informal votes cannot properly be taken during a meeting.

No body, board, or committee can, during its meeting, properly take a vote that is not binding. If an assembly wishes to vote to recess to determine the probable vote of the members, it may do so; but under the law all votes taken during a meeting are binding.

Chapter 18

NOMINATIONS AND ELECTIONS

Choosing Organization Leaders

The process of nominating and electing officers is vital to every organization, because the abilities and talents of the leaders largely determine the achievements of the group.

Parliamentary law permits a wide latitude of choice in each step of the nominating and electing process. There is no one perfect method, but there are certain procedures that experience has proved are better than others for obtaining good leaders.

Bylaw Provisions on Nominations and Elections

The bylaw provisions on nominations should include the offices to be filled, the eligibility and qualifications of candidates, the method and time of nominating, and the term of office. If a nominating committee is to be used, provisions for selecting its members and determining their qualifications, instructions, duties, and reporting should also be included.

The bylaw provisions on elections should include the time, place, and method of voting, the notice required, a statement of who is eligible to vote, the vote required to elect, the method of conducting the election, and the time when the new officers take office. Some bylaws include a provision for special elections if needed to fill vacancies.

Nominations from the Floor

A nomination is the formal presentation to an assembly of the name of a member as a candidate for a particular office. If the bylaws do not provide the method for nominating officers, any member may propose a motion determining how nominations are to be made.

Unless the bylaws provide otherwise, nominations from the floor are always permitted even if the initial nominations are made by a nominating committee. To open nominations the presiding officer may say: "Are there nominations [or further nominations] for the office of president?" Any member may then rise and say, for example, "I nominate Mary Smith."

It is customary in some organizations to permit a nominator to give reasons for supporting the nominee. Nominations do not require seconds, but some organizations permit other members to give endorsing statements, which are called "seconding speeches." If the report of a nominating committee states the qualifications and abilities of its nominees, a member who nominates from the floor may also state the qualifications and abilities of the candidate.

The presiding officer should repeat the request for further nominations and should pause to allow ample opportunity for members to present nominees. When there appear to be no further nominations for a particular office, the chair may declare nominations for that office closed, or ask for nominations for the next office without closing nominations; or some member may move that nominations for that office be closed. The presiding officer should not recognize a motion to close nominations or declare them closed, however, until members have had a reasonable opportunity to nominate.

A motion to close nominations or a declaration by the presiding officer closing nominations is not required. If nominations have been closed, they may be reopened by a motion to this effect until voting has begun.

Relying solely on nominations from the floor is usually not the most satisfactory method for securing the best candidates. The lack of time for considering qualifications, the tendency of nominees to decline nominations from the floor, and the resulting confusion often prevent the organization from securing the best leaders. A nominating committee, so long as it is fairly chosen and is representative, will usually select good candidates, but nominations from the floor should always be provided for as a safeguard.

Voting for Candidates Not Nominated

A member need not be nominated for an office, either from the floor or by a committee, to be elected to that office when the vote is taken by ballot or by roll call. Members may vote for anyone who is eligible, regardless of whether the person has been nominated, by writing in the name of their choice on the ballot or voting for that person on roll call. Any member receiving the necessary vote is elected, whether nominated or not. The member does, of course, have the right to decline the office.

Selecting a Nominating Committee

A nominating committee is one of the most important committees of an organization because it can help to secure the best officers. Nomination of candidates by a committee has advantages. A committee has the time to study the leadership needs of the organization and to select candidates to meet these needs. It can interview prospective nominees; investigate their experience, qualifications, and abilities; persuade them to become candidates; and secure their consent to serve if elected. The committee is also able to apportion representation equitably among different groups and different areas.

A nominating committee should be a representative committee. Many organizations provide, for example, that if the nominating committee consists of five members, three of the members are elected by the membership, and the chairman and the fifth member are appointed by the governing board.

The members chosen by the board are usually current or recent members of the board who, by reason of their service, have a broad and up-to-date knowledge of the needs of the organization and of the leadership abilities of its members. The members of the committee elected by the membership usually reflect the viewpoint of the general membership.

Any plan by which experienced leaders choose some of the members of the nominating committee and the membership chooses the other members is usually effective in securing a committee that is both representative and knowledgeable.

The president should not appoint any members of the nominating committee, serve on the committee, give the committee instructions, or take any part in its deliberations. This requirement protects both the president and the committee from accusations of favoritism or self-perpetuation.

When a nominating committee is used, it is essential that the members be chosen wisely and democratically and that both the committee and the membership be protected by permitting nominations from the floor.

Duties of a Nominating Committee

A carefully chosen nominating committee should be permitted to use its judgment in selecting the candidates who will give the best service to the organization. It should choose the candidates on the basis of what is good for all the members and not on the basis that an office is a reward to be given to a deserving member. The committee may invite suggestions but should not be limited by them.

A few organizations use the nominating committee merely as a computing group to which names from various areas or local groups are sent and the results tabulated. This type of committee does little more than compile a list of nominees based on the preferences stated by the various areas or local groups.

On the other hand, many organizations believe that the best leaders are secured by delegating to the nominating committee the duty to find and nominate the best candidates. The duties usually assigned to such a nominating committee are:

1. To study the problems and leadership requirements of the organization. For example, if the organization has financial difficulties, dissension, or a decreasing membership, it needs leaders who are capable of solving such problems. The particular needs of the organization for the next term of office may be summarized in an introduction to the report of the nominating committee.

2. To select nominees who have the experience and the qualities that meet the needs of the organization.

3. To interview prospective nominees personally, by telephone, or by mail, and secure their consent to serve if elected.

4. To prepare a report containing the committee's analysis of the leadership needs of the organization, the names of the nominees, their experience and qualifications, and the reasons that the committee feels the candidates named can meet these needs.

5. To submit its report to the meeting or convention and for publication and distribution to the members.

Qualifications of Nominees

Qualifications for each office should be stated in the bylaws. No member who lacks the qualifications specified in the bylaws can be a candidate for, or be elected to, an office. The nomination of an unqualified member must be ruled out of order.

Nomination to More Than One Office

No member can accept nomination for or hold two incompatible offices. Some organizations in their bylaws combine two offices, thus, in effect, declaring them compatible. For example, the offices of secretary and treasurer are sometimes combined as secretary-treasurer. Membership on the governing board is usually compatible with other offices such as president or secretary. The fact that bylaws usually provide that the officers serve on the board is a determination of compatibility. Incompatibility does not consist of physical impossibility to perform the duties of both offices but lies in a conflict of interest between the duties of the two offices.

A member who is nominated for two incompatible offices at the same election must choose which office to run for, and decline the other nomination. Unless the bylaws provide otherwise, a member who holds an office may be a candidate for another office, but if the member is elected to and accepts an incompatible office, the former office is forfeited.

Nominating Committee Members
as Candidates

Members who are likely to become candidates should not serve on a nominating committee. But members of the committee can become candidates. If they were barred from becoming candidates, supporters of one candidate might maneuver to place prospective opponents on the nominating committee in order to disqualify them from candidacy. A member of a nominating committee who becomes a candidate should resign from the committee immediately.

Single and Multiple Slate

If an organization chooses a representative nominating committee carefully and democratically, it may be desirable to nominate a single candidate for each office. A single slate, meaning one nominee for each office, frequently offers certain advantages provided that nominations may also be made from the floor and that election by write-in votes is not forbidden.

In some organizations the belief persists that it is more democratic to have two or more nominees for each office in order that there may be a contest. This belief is probably based on the fact that national and state governments have a two-party political system and therefore have a candidate from each party for each office. But there is a growing tendency for nongovernmental organizations to nominate a single slate.

There are many capable members who may be persuaded to take the responsibility of an office if they believe that the membership wishes them to do so. But often they will not engage in a contest with other members for the office.

When a nominating committee is required to submit the names of two or more nominees for each office, it often faces a dilemma. If the committee members decide, for example, that candidate A can offer the best leadership as president, they are obliged to do either of two things. They may add another nominee who is not well qualified in the hope that candidate A will be more certain to be elected, or they may add regretfully the name of candidate B who is also well qualified, and sacrifice one of their two best potential leaders by defeat.

Defeated candidates seldom choose to run again. Thus, the services of many good leaders may be lost to the organization because they are sacrificed to furnish a contest. Few organizations can afford this waste of good leadership. There is no particular democratic purpose served by nominating several members in order to defeat all but one of them.

In organizations that provide for a single slate, there are situations that make a contest for an office necessary or desirable. For example, if the members are seeking to decide an important policy or course of action and they do not wish to vote on the matter directly, they may decide it by nominating two or more candidates who represent substantially different opinions and then voting on the candidates. Such an election is not simply a vote for the best-qualified candidate for the office but is a vote to decide on the course of future action and on a candidate who is best qualified to carry out that action.

The single slate always should be safeguarded by the right of nominations from the floor and of write-in votes. If the nominating committee fails to express the will of the majority of the members in its selection of nominees, this should be rectified by adding nominees from the floor to provide a contest.

Election Committee

Organizations usually appoint an election committee which conducts the election. This committee should also be a representative committee. It supervises the preparation and printing of ballots, their distribution to voting members either at a meeting or convention or by mail, the collection and counting of the ballots, and the preparation of a report showing the results of the election.

Counting Ballots

The election committee is generally responsible for seeing that ballots are counted accurately. One effective method of counting ballots is for one member to read the votes for all offices from each ballot while another member stands near enough to check the correctness of the reading. The votes are recorded by another member whose tabulation is also checked to ensure accuracy. If a ballot has several offices to be voted upon, it is more efficient to divide the recording of the votes between two or more teams of recorders and checkers, each recording only the votes for one or two offices. While counting the votes, there should be silence except for the reading of the names. If there is a possible error, some member says, "Stop," and the vote is verified before proceeding.

In large organizations, where thousands of votes must be counted, the ballots are divided among many teams of readers, counters, and checkers and counted in the same way by each team. Votes are usually tallied in groups of five. Any member has a right to be present while the ballots are being counted.

Many organizations have developed effective methods of counting ballots, to meet their own needs. Any method is appropriate if it is accurate.

Determining Legality of Ballots

The legality of ballots is governed by the following rules:

1. A mistake in voting for a candidate for one office does not invalidate the vote for candidates for other offices on the same ballot.

2. A technical error, such as misspelling, or using a cross instead of a check, does not invalidate a ballot if the *intent* of the voter is clear.

3. A torn or defaced ballot is valid if the *intent* of the voter is clear.

4. Blank ballots or votes for ineligible persons are counted as illegal ballots.

5. If several nominees for equal offices (for example, members of a governing board) are voted for in a group, a ballot containing fewer votes than the number of positions to be filled is valid. But a ballot containing votes for more than the number of positions to be filled is illegal for all the positions.

If the results of the count by the committee do not check, a recount must be made. If more ballots have been cast than there are members entitled to vote, and the result of the election could have been affected by the extra ballots, or if there has been any substantial violation of the right of members to vote in secret, the vote must be retaken. If there are minor errors which could not change the result of the election, a vote need not be retaken.

Report of Election Committee or Tellers

The following example shows the essential requirements of a report of an election committee:

REPORT OF ELECTION COMMITTEE
January 19
SACRAMENTO FARM BUREAU

Qualified voters	340
Legal ballots cast	338
Illegal ballots rejected (ballots were blank)	2

President

Legal votes cast for president	330
Illegal votes (cast for ineligible person)	1
Number of votes necessary to elect	166
Candidate A received	323
Candidate B received (write-in votes)	7

Secretary

Legal votes cast for secretary	338
Number necessary to elect	170
Candidate D received	336
Candidate E received (write-in votes)	2

Board of Trustees (three to be elected)

Number of legal ballots cast for trustees	331
Number of votes necessary to elect	166
Candidate F received	326
Candidate G received	318
Candidate H received	315
Candidate I received (write-in votes)	13

Signatures of Committee

The report must account for all ballots cast, both legal and illegal. If any ballots or votes are rejected as illegal, the number must be reported and the reasons for rejection must be given. The number of votes received by each candidate and the number of write-in votes for any member, qualified or unqualified, must be included in the report and must be read.

The chairman of the election committee reads the report without stating who is elected and hands it to the presiding officer. The presiding officer reads only the names of those who are elected and declares them elected.

The report is signed by all members of the election committee. Tally sheets are signed by those who kept them. All ballots, tally sheets, and records are delivered to the secretary of the organization who keeps them sealed until directed by the governing board to destroy them.

Vote Necessary to Elect

The vote necessary to elect should be fixed in the bylaws. Unless otherwise provided, the following rules govern:

1. A candidate who receives a majority of the legal votes cast for a single office is elected.

2. A candidate who receives a plurality of the legal votes cast (more votes than any other candidate), but not a majority, is not elected unless there is a provision in the bylaws for election by plurality.

3. When election to an office requires a majority vote, but no candidate receives a majority vote, the requirement for a majority vote cannot be waived but the assembly may adopt motions to enable it to complete the election within a reasonable time. (See *Supplementing Procedural Rules by Motions,* p. 200.)

Casting of Ballot by the Secretary

Most bylaws provide for the election of officers by ballot vote. When there is only one candidate for an office or a slate consisting of one candidate for each office, or when additional votes are necessary to secure a majority vote as required for an office, a member sometimes proposes a motion that the secretary be instructed to cast the ballot of the members for the candidate or slate. This motion deprives members of their right to write in the name of another member and to keep their choice secret, since they cannot oppose this motion without revealing that they favor some other member. But it does save considerable time. If an organization wishes to provide that the secretary may be directed to cast a ballot for the assembly, this provision should be included in its bylaws. Unless the bylaws provide for the casting of a ballot for an uncontested candidate, the general provision requiring a ballot vote for all officers must be complied with.

The motion directing the secretary to cast a ballot, when permitted, requires a majority vote. It should not be stated as a motion "to cast a unanimous ballot," since this would require a unanimous vote.

If the motion for the secretary to cast a ballot carries, the secretary prepares a ballot as directed and, rising, says, "Mr. President, by direction of the members I cast the ballot of the members for candidate A for the office of president and for candidates C and D for members of the board of directors." Then the presiding officer declares these members elected.

Motion to Make a Vote Unanimous

A unanimous vote means that all of the legal votes cast were cast on one side and that there were no votes cast on the other side. One common error is to suppose that a vote which is not unanimous can be made unanimous by adopting a motion to that effect by majority vote. Sometimes the candidate receiving the second highest number of votes or one of that candidate's supporters proposes a motion to make the vote unanimous for the elected candidate. This is only a complimentary gesture, and does not change the legal vote.

When Elections Become Effective

An election becomes effective immediately if the candidate is present and does not decline. Election of a candidate who is absent and has consented to nomination becomes effective as soon as the person is notified. Unless some other time is specified in the bylaws, an officer assumes office when declared elected, and no formal installation is necessary.

Sometimes the bylaws provide that the new officers should take office at a later date. The ceremony of installing officers does not determine the time at which they assume office unless the bylaws contain a provision that the new officers take office at the time of their installation.

Challenging a Vote

A member who desires to challenge the right of another member or members to vote, or the validity of a proxy, should do so by presenting the challenge to the credentials committee or to the election committee. This should be done before the voting has begun or at least before the challenged vote is cast. If the right of a member to vote is challenged, the credentials committee or the election committee holds a hearing and decides the matter subject to an appeal to the assembly. If there is no election committee, a challenge is decided by the assembly.

Challenging an Election

An election may be challenged only during the time that it is taking place or within a reasonably brief time thereafter. The grounds for challenging an election are usually that persons who are ineligible have voted, that procedures required for carrying out a fair election were not observed, that procedures or actions during the election were unauthorized or illegal, that there was gross negligence in conducting the election, or that the election requirements in the bylaws were not correctly interpreted or followed and that these violations could have changed the result of the election.

When an election is challenged, an investigation is usually made by the board of directors or by a committee selected by them, or by the elections committee. The board or committee reports its recommendation to the meeting or convention for final decision. If the meeting or convention is no longer in session, the board of directors decides the matter and takes whatever action seems best. The board must report its action to the members.

When an election is challenged while it is in progress, it continues unless a decision is reached to stop the election and declare it void. If it is challenged after it is completed, the officers chosen at the election take office and remain in office until a decision on the challenge is reached.

If it can be proved that enough illegal votes were cast so that the results of the election could have been changed, the election should be voided. If illegal votes cast or illegal practices engaged in could not have changed the results of the election, the fact that there were illegal votes or practices does not void the election.

Chapter 19

OFFICERS

The President as Leader

The president or the head of an organization, whatever the title may be, usually has three roles—leader, administrator, and presiding officer. Each role calls for different abilities.

There are certain fundamental qualities that most good leaders have in common. One is the *ability to plan*—to sense what the members want and to help them crystallize their ideas. Another is the *ability to unite*—to rally members behind a plan and behind their leader. Perhaps the most important is the *courage to win*—to overcome all obstacles.

A good leader works with the members, and keeps them happy while they are working. Such a leader has a power *with* people, not *over* them. Carrying out their will is a project in human collaboration, which the president leads.

An organization is not merely a group of people working toward some common aim. It is also a powerful medium through which members can realize their individual hopes. A competent leader forges ahead toward the collective goal, but is not blind to individual aims.

A leader skilled in handling people recognizes that sentiment and tradition are important influences, both in welding people together and in dividing them. This human understanding is a basic factor in good leadership.

The President as Administrator

The most important duties of the president as administrator are those that follow.

1. Act as chief administrative officer and legal head of the organization

2. Exercise supervision over the organization and all its activities and employees

3. Represent and speak for the organization to other organizations and to the public

4. Preside at business meetings

5. Appoint committees

6. Sign letters or documents necessary to carry out the will of the organization

7. Preside at meetings of the board of directors or governing board

The President as Presiding Officer

As presiding officer the president is the leader and representative of the entire assembly. Respect for this position is respect for the organization. The president must maintain firm control of the meeting, yet always must act primarily as "the first servant of the assembly."

Just as a judge exercises wide discretion in a courtroom, the presiding officer should exercise wide discretion in a meeting. Instead of being limited to mechanical responses, the president must meet each situation with flexibility of judgment, common sense, and fairness to all members, acting always impartially and in good faith. For example, if a member moves to adjourn, and the presiding officer knows that there is important business that should be attended to, this should be explained to the member, who may then withdraw the motion. If the member refuses, the presiding officer should explain the business that needs attention before the vote on adjournment is taken.

During discussion, the presiding officer has great latitude in assisting members in exercising their rights and privileges. Although the presiding officer should not act as a partisan advocate, it is appropriate to state facts of which others may not be aware, provided this is done in an unbiased manner. The president should stimulate and encourage discussion, and should see that all sides of a controversial question are presented by asking if members wish to discuss a different viewpoint and by alternating the opportunity to speak between friends and foes of the question.

The president should make sure that members understand all proposals and what their effect will be.

A presiding officer should protect the group from improper conduct, and should warn obstructionists who are using dilatory tactics; if they persist, he or she should deny them recognition. The presiding officer should expose parliamentary trickery, prevent railroading, and promptly rule out discussion of personalities.

A presiding officer must be firm and decisive, yet not dictatorial; courteous and patient, yet alert to ensure progress.

Presiding is an art that cannot be learned entirely from a book. The tactful presiding officer knows how to discourage courteously the member who talks too much or too often and how to encourage the shy member who speaks only when impelled by strong convictions. When an assembly is restive, a good presiding officer knows how to shorten discussion and how to make business move along, but senses when members are confused and when the business should move more slowly.

Above all, a good presiding officer must have a working knowledge of parliamentary procedure and how to apply it.

Associate Justice Felix Frankfurter described the ideal presiding officer when he wrote (of Chief Justice Charles Evans Hughes):

> He presided with great courtesy and with a quiet authority... with great but gentle firmness. You couldn't but catch his own mood of courtesy.
>
> He never checked free debate, but the atmosphere which he created, the moral authority which he exerted, inhibited irrelevance, repetition, and fruitless discussion.
>
> He was a master of timing: he knew when discussion should be deferred and when brought to an issue. He also showed uncommon resourcefulness in drawing elements of agreement out of differences, and thereby narrowing, if not always escaping, conflicts.[1]

When the President Presides

The president, or in the absence of the president the officer next in rank, should preside at all meetings at which business may be transacted. If no officers are present at a meeting, a senior member calls the meeting to order and presides until a temporary chairman is elected. At social or program meetings, the program chairman or another member may preside; but at business meetings the president, if present, must preside, and cannot delegate this duty to another member without permission from the assembly.

If the president wishes to participate in debate on a controversial question, the chair should be turned over temporarily to the vice president or some other ranking officer who has not expressed an opinion. Or, if the other officers also prefer to participate in the discussion, the chair may be turned over to some other impartial member. If there is controversy over the person so designated, the matter is settled by a vote, with the person named by the president being considered one of the nominees for the temporary chairmanship.

The presiding officer does not leave the chair merely to present important facts that need to be presented. However, if a motion is directed at the president personally, the vice president is asked to take the chair until action on the motion has been completed. This is true whether the motion affects the president favorably—such as, for example, to award a life membership—or adversely, as a vote of censure.

Although there is a general principle that a person does not give up any basic rights as a member by becoming an officer, the presiding officer of an assembly cannot propose or second a motion or nominate a candidate while presiding. However, the president does preside during an election even when he or she is a candidate for office.

The President-elect

Some organizations elect a future president as much as a year before the term of office begins, and in the interim period assign specific duties which will increase that person's familiarity with the workings of the organization. The president-elect is in training for the office of president and automatically becomes the president when the latter's term of office expires.

The president-elect usually assumes the duties of the president when that officer is absent or is incapacitated. The president-elect also presides when it is necessary for the president to leave the chair, unless the bylaws specify that the vice president should do so.

When acting in the place of the president, the president-elect has all the powers, duties, responsibilities, and privileges of the president.

The Vice President

The vice president assumes the duties of the president in case of the absence or incapacity of the president and becomes president on the death, resignation, or permanent incapacity of the president unless the bylaws provide differently.

The vice president has only a few responsibilities established by parliamentary law, but in practice is usually assigned other duties by the bylaws. Vice presidents frequently direct departments of work or study, head important committees, serve on the governing board, and have other duties assigned to them.

The Secretary

The president and the elected secretary are recognized by the law as the legal representatives of the organization. The secretary has extensive duties, serving as the chief recording and corresponding officer and the custodian of the records of the organization. In organizations in which employees perform these functions, the responsibility for seeing that they are properly carried out remains with the elected secretary. The secretary works under the direction of the president.

The chief duties of a secretary are to:

1. Take careful and authentic notes of the proceedings of the meetings as a basis for preparing the minutes

2. Prepare and certify the correctness of the minutes and enter them in the official minute book

3. Read the minutes to the organization for correction and approval

4. Enter any corrections approved by the members in the minute book and initial them

5. Record the approved minutes as the official minutes of the organization, with the date of their approval, signing them to attest to their validity

6. Provide the presiding officer or the assembly with the exact wording of a pending motion or of one previously acted on

7. Prepare a list of members and call the roll when directed by the presiding officer

8. Read all papers, documents, or communications as directed by the presiding officer

9. Bring to each meeting the minute book; a copy of the bylaws, rules, and policies; a list of the members; a list of standing and special committees; and a copy of the parliamentary authority adopted by the organization

10. Search the minutes for information requested by officers or members

11. Assist the presiding officer before each meeting in preparing a detailed agenda

12. Preserve all records, reports, and official documents of the organization except those specifically assigned to the custody of others

13. Prepare and send required notices of meetings and proposals

14. Provide the chairman of each special committee with a list of the committee members, a copy of the motion referring the subject to the committee, and instructions and other documents that may be useful

15. Provide the chairman of each standing committee with a copy of all proposals referred to it, instructions, or material that may be useful

16. Sign official documents to attest to their authenticity

17. Carry on the official correspondence of the organization as directed, except correspondence assigned to other officers

In addition to these duties, the secretary performs many lesser tasks such as calling attention to actions in the minutes that have not been carried out, and keeping a report book or file of all reports submitted, a correspondence file, and a book of adopted policies and procedures. The secretary is responsible for calling attention to deadlines and the dates for taking certain actions.

The elected secretary does not forfeit any rights of membership by reason of holding office, and may propose motions and discuss and vote on all measures.

The Corresponding Secretary

In some organizations the secretarial duties are divided between a recording secretary and a corresponding secretary. The corresponding secretary conducts the official correspondence for the organization as directed by the president or board, answers official letters, and maintains a correspondence file.

The Treasurer

The treasurer is responsible for the collection, safekeeping, and expenditure of all funds of the organization, and for keeping an accurate financial record. The treasurer should be a person of unquestioned integrity and should have a knowledge of how to keep, or supervise the keeping of, financial accounts.

In organizations that delegate to employees the work of collecting, disbursing, and accounting for funds, the treasurer is still legally responsible for the performance of these duties and for the accuracy of the treasurer's reports.

The treasurer collects and disburses funds only as directed by law, the bylaws, the membership, the board of directors, or other authority provided for in the bylaws. The treasurer does not have the power to borrow money or issue funds or checks except as authorized to do so by the assembly or bylaws. The treasurer usually has the responsibility of helping to prepare the budget.

The treasurer should report briefly on the finances of the organization at each membership and board meeting, answer any questions on financial matters, and submit a full report to the membership annually. (See *Report of the Treasurer*, p. 203.)

The Member Parliamentarian

There are two types of parliamentarians. One is the employed consultant who has had training and professional experience in parliamentary law and who is not a member of the organization. (See *The Parliamentarian*, p. 219.)

The other is the parliamentarian appointed from the membership by the president. The member parliamentarian should be a source of information on parliamentary procedure, but, like all parliamentarians, has no authority to make rulings or to enforce them.

A component member parliamentarian can be a valuable aid to the presiding officer and to the other officers and members.

The Sergeant-at-Arms

The sergeant-at-arms, under the direction of the presiding officer, helps to maintain order and decorum at meetings. The sergeant-at-arms acts as doorkeeper, directs the ushers, and is responsible for the comfort and convenience of the assembly. In small organizations these duties are performed by one person, but in a large one there may be a staff of assistant sergeants-at-arms.

Honorary Officers

Some organizations provide in their bylaws for honorary officers and members. Honorary titles are created as a compliment to those on whom they are conferred; such honorary titles generally carry with them the right to attend meetings and to speak but not to propose motions, vote, or preside. Holding an honorary office does not prevent a person who is a member from exercising any rights or from holding a regular office.

Powers and Liabilities of Officers

The actual powers and duties of officers are stated in the bylaws and sometimes in statutes and charters. In addition, officers have the implied power to do whatever is necessary to carry out the functions and duties of their office. For example, a president who has the duty of appointing a committee has the implied power to fill a vacancy on the committee or to remove and replace a committee member who fails to perform prescribed duties.

Delegation of Authority by Officers and Boards

Both officers and members should understand their responsibilities in delegating to other members or employees the powers, duties, and responsibilities assigned to them by the law or the bylaws.

The basic principle of the delegation of powers, duties, and responsibilities is that the members, officers, boards, or committees delegating authority retain full responsibility for the performance or exercise of the powers, duties, and responsibilities that they have delegated. They also are responsible for negligence and its consequences in the exercise of the delegated authority.

There are two general types of powers, duties, and responsibilities—legislative and administrative. *Legislative* powers and duties provided for by statute or bylaws, either expressly or by implication, cannot be delegated, except in profit-making corporations where most duties are delegated to the board. For example, if the bylaws provide that an organization elect its officers by a ballot vote of the delegates at the annual convention, the assembly of delegates cannot delegate this duty to its board of directors.

Administrative powers and duties are of two kinds—discretionary and ministerial. *Discretionary* powers and duties are those that depend on a special trust in the officer, board, or committee member and involve personal reliance on that person's wisdom, integrity, and discretion. An example of a discretionary duty is the appointment of committees by the president or the certification of minutes by the secretary.

Discretionary powers and duties assigned to a particular officer or board by statute, charter, or bylaws can never be delegated. For example, a board of directors of a nonprofit corporation cannot delegate its power to borrow money. The board of directors can authorize a committee or an employee to investigate the best rates and sources for borrowing money, but the final decision must be made by the board.

Ministerial powers or duties are those that require simply carrying out specifically described duties that do not call for the use of discretion but involve only the faithful performance of a mechanical or clerical function. Ministerial powers and duties can be delegated freely to members or employees. For example, a secretary has the ministerial duty of sending out notices of a meeting already authorized and can delegate this duty to members or employees.

A committee may delegate some of its powers and duties to a subcommittee, but the committee remains responsible for all actions of its subcommittees.

Powers and duties should be delegated carefully and with the knowledge that the responsibility for supervising their exercise and execution remains with those making the delegation.

Term of Office

The bylaws should define the term of office of all officers, directors, and committees. Bylaws sometimes limit the number of terms that a member may hold an office. This provision is intended to prevent domination of the organization by a few members. However, a limitation on terms often works out to be more a limitation on the right of members to elect whom they please than a limitation on a member to continue to hold office. The deciding principle should be, not the right of every member to have "a turn" regardless of ability, but the overall good of the organization.

Many organizations favor a short term of office, which brings officers up for review by election frequently. If the members are alert and interested, it is often unnecessary and disadvantageous to limit the number of terms to which a member may be elected, because "one year is too long for a poor officer and too short for a good one."

When there is a provision in the bylaws restricting the number of terms to which a member may be elected to a particular office, a member who fills a vacancy in that office for a partial term is not barred from being elected to a full term or terms, unless the bylaws provide otherwise.

When eligibility to hold a certain office includes a requirement that a member must have served a term in another office, serving for half or more of a term to fill a vacancy ordinarily fulfills the requirement.

Officers are not always elected with the regularity or at the precise time prescribed by law or the bylaws. The ordinary rule in such cases is that the incumbents continue to hold office until their successors are elected or appointed.

Vacancies

The bylaws should include rules governing vacancies. A vacancy in an office, board, or committee usually occurs because of the death, resignation, or departure of the member from the locality, and in these instances there is no question that a vacancy exists.

There is sometimes uncertainty when a vacancy occurs by reason of discovery of the ineligibility of an officer after the person has been elected, or when there has been an abandonment of the office, an implied resignation, or prolonged neglect or inability to act. If there is a question as to whether an office is vacant, the board or the members should declare the office vacant to clear the record before a member is chosen to fill the vacancy.

Declaring a vacancy is not a means of removing an officer. An office cannot be declared vacant when there is an incumbent willing and able to perform the duties of the office.

A vacancy is filled by the same authority that selected the officer, director, or committee member unless the bylaws provide otherwise. A special election is sometimes called to enable the members to fill a vacancy.

Some bylaws provide that the officer who is next in rank automatically moves up to fill a vacancy. Other bylaws require the board of directors to fill vacancies not otherwise provided for. If this duty is delegated to the directors or to any other group except the membership, the member chosen to fill the vacancy serves only until the next election at which the vacancy can be filled by the membership.

Vacancies in elective offices must not be ignored or concealed. Members should be informed promptly of a vacancy, and the vacancy should be filled as soon as possible. If the board of directors or the president knows that there is, or is about to be, a vacancy, this knowledge cannot properly be withheld until after a meeting, convention, or election at which the members could have elected someone to fill the vacancy; to do so would permit the president or board to fill the vacancy by appointment.

Neither officers nor members should try to outwit the provisions of the bylaws by maneuvering to fill vacancies in elective offices by appointment. No member should accept an elective office with the intention of resigning in order to create a vacancy and thereby permit the appointment of another member to the office.

Removal of Officers

An organization has an inherent right to remove an officer or director from office for valid cause. It also has the right to suspend an officer or director from office. The bylaws should provide for procedures for removal or suspension. These procedures are quite different from those for the disciplining or expulsion of a member.

Officers, directors, or committee members can be removed by the same authority that selected them. The power to select carries with it the power to remove. An elected officer or director can be removed by vote of the members. An appointed officer or committee member can be removed by the authority that made the appointment.

The common *valid* causes for removal from office are:

1. Continued, gross, or willful neglect of the duties of the office

2. Failure or refusal to disclose necessary information on matters of organization business

3. Unauthorized expenditures, signing of checks, or misuse of organization funds

4. Unwarranted attacks on the president or refusal to cooperate with the president

5. Misrepresentation of the organization and its officers to outside persons

6. Conviction of a felony

Examples of conduct that are *not valid* grounds for removal from office are:

1. Poor performance as an officer due to lack of ability

2. Negligence that is not gross or willful

3. A tendency to create friction and disagreement

4. Mere unsuitability to hold office

The procedures for suspending or removing officers must provide adequate notice to the accused officer, a fair hearing, the right to counsel, and a reasonable opportunity for the officer to present a defense.

An officer who complains of improper removal or a member who believes that he or she has been disciplined improperly must exhaust the procedures for relief afforded by the organization before appealing to the courts. If proper procedures are followed, the courts will seldom interfere with the removal of an officer for valid cause.

Chapter 20

COMMITTEES AND BOARDS

Importance of Committees

Committees perform the bulk of the work of organizations. Through the use of committees the responsibilities of an organization are apportioned among its members. Work to be done is delegated to committees and proposals are formulated by committees for final decision by the whole assembly. The meetings of many groups are concerned largely with the consideration of committee reports and recommendations. Usually the conclusions of committees are accepted as the conclusions of the organization.

Committees are too valuable to be misused. They should not be burial grounds for unpleasant issues, or a method of rewarding members and distributing titles to friends, or a device for giving everybody something to do. Membership on a committee should never be used to placate chronic troublemakers.

No committee should be appointed unless it is needed. Members of a committee that has no real work soon recognize this fact and lose interest in the organization.

Advantages of Committees

A committee has many advantages that enable it to work more efficiently than the larger parent organization. Some of these are that:

1. Greater freedom of discussion is possible.
2. More time is available for each subject.

3. Informal procedure can be used.

4. Better use can be made of experts and consultants.

5. Delicate and troublesome questions may be settled without publicity.

6. Hearings may be held giving members opportunity to express their opinions.

Standing Committees

A standing committee does any work within its particular field that is assigned to it by the bylaws or referred to it by the organization or the board. Its term of service is usually the same as the terms of the officers. Standing committees provide ever-ready and experienced groups to which work may be referred at any time. They handle many tasks that need to be carried out regularly. A membership committee, which investigates and passes on applications for membership, is an example of a standing committee.

An organization may provide for and fix the duties of as many standing committees as it finds useful. The name, method of selecting members, usual duties, term of office, and requirements for reports of each standing committee should be included in the bylaws.

Special Committees

A special committee, sometimes called an *ad hoc* committee, performs some specific task and automatically ceases to exist when its final report is issued. If the organization votes to delegate additional work to a special committee, it continues until the new assignment is completed and another report is submitted. A committee to arrange the annual banquet is an example of a special committee.

Both the board of directors and the president have the inherent power to appoint special committees to assist them at any time, and to delegate investigative, planning, or routine administrative duties to them. These committees report only to the authority that appointed them. (See *Delegation of Authority by Officers and Boards*, p. 161.)

Committees for Deliberation

Committees may be classified according to the nature of their assignments into committees primarily for deliberation and committees primarily for action. It is vital that a committee appointed for deliberation and investigation or which performs discretionary duties be representative of all important elements and groups within the organization. The report of a representative committee will reflect the opinions of the whole organization and has a good chance of being approved. A nominating committee and a committee to determine the location for a new clubhouse are examples of committees that should be representative.

Committees for Action

A committee for action carries out a particular task already decided on. Such a committee does not function well unless it is composed of members who favor the job to be done. A committee to raise an endowment fund is an example.

Selection of the Committee Chairman

A committee chairman should be chosen for the ability to plan and direct the work of the committee and to function well with its members. Unlike the presiding officer of an assembly, the chairman of a committee takes an active part in its discussion and deliberations.

If no committee chairman is elected or appointed, a chairman may be selected by the committee from its own membership. If no chairman is designated, the member first named calls the committee together and presides during the election of a chairman. There is no parliamentary rule requiring that the member who proposes the creation of a committee be appointed as chairman or member of it, and there is no rule barring such appointment.

Selection of the Committee Members

Members of standing committees are usually appointed by the president with the approval of the governing board. The advice and suggestions of board members enable the president to utilize the talents of a larger number of members effectively.

It is often advisable to consult a prospective committee chairman regarding the selection of the other committee members, particularly if the committee has a difficult assignment.

Ex Officio Members of Committees

The bylaws of some organizations provide that the president or other officers, because of the particular office they hold, are automatically members of certain boards or committees. Such members are termed "ex officio" members. An ex officio member is not elected or appointed to a committee, but becomes a member when elected or appointed to a particular office. When an ex officio member ceases to hold office, that person's membership on the committee terminates, and the new holder of the office assumes the ex officio membership. The president and other officers are usually ex officio members of the board of directors. The treasurer is usually an ex officio member of the finance committee.

An ex officio member has all the rights, responsibilities, and duties of any other member of the committee, including the right to vote. An ex officio member is not, as is commonly believed, merely a consulting or advising member, but is a full-fledged working member of the committee. Consequently a president cannot be expected to serve effectively as an ex officio member of all committees. If it is desirable to have the president or some other officer act only as a consultant or adviser to a particular committee, that person should be made an advisory or consulting member rather than an ex officio member.

Powers, Rights, and Duties of Committees

The powers, rights, and duties of each standing committee and of important special committees that are appointed periodically should be provided for in the bylaws. The powers, rights, and duties of other special committees should be provided for in the motion creating them or in the instructions given to them. Since no committee has inherent powers, rights, or duties, these must be delegated to it by the creating or appointing authority. Even an executive committee or board of directors has no powers and no duties except those delegated to it by the bylaws or by vote of the membership. (See *Delegation of Authority by Officers and Boards,* p. 161.)

All committees are responsible to and under the direction and control of the authority that created them. Standing committees are responsible to and under the control of the voting body and the governing board when it is acting for the voting body in the intervals between meetings. Special committees appointed by the membership, the governing board, or the president are responsible to the appointing authority.

Any subject or duty that has been assigned to a committee may be withdrawn at any time and assigned to another committee or considered by the body. Any proposal or assignment of work to a standing committee may be withdrawn by the governing body unless it is assigned exclusively to the committee by the bylaws. Any special committee may be dissolved by the authority that created it.

The members of a committee may be replaced by the appointing or electing authority. A member of a committee who is unable or fails to participate in committee activities should be removed and notified of the removal by the president or by the body that appointed the committee, and another member should be chosen to fill the vacancy.

A committee cannot represent the organization to any outside person or organization except when clearly authorized to do so. Unless there is specific authorization given a committee to collect, hold, or disburse funds, all funds should be collected, held, and disbursed through the regular financial channels of the organization.

A committee has the right to appoint subcommittees of its own members to which it may delegate authority and which are directly responsible to the committee. Subcommittees report only to the committee that created them.

Working Materials for Committees

The secretary should furnish each committee with specific instructions on the work it is expected to do, and with all helpful information in the possession of the organization, such as:

1. A list for each member of the committee members with addresses and telephone numbers

2. A statement of the motion, problem, or task referred to the committee

3. Any instructions to the committee from the membership, governing board, or president

4. A statement of the duties, powers, and financial limitations of the committee

5. Available information that will be helpful to the committee—for example, reports of former similar committees

6. Policies, rules, or decisions of the organizations relating to the committee's work

7. The nature of the report desired and the date it is due

It is the duty of the secretary of the organization to provide these materials for each committee. If the secretary of the organization does not provide such materials, it is the duty of the chairman of the committee to obtain them for the committee members.

Committee Meetings Limited to Members

Since committees and boards of directors often consider business of a confidential nature, which should not be discussed at a meeting of the membership, the privacy of a committee must be protected. No officer, member, employee, or outside person has the right to attend any meeting of a board or committee except by invitation of the committee.

If the committee wishes to invite a staff member, consultant, or other person, it may vote to do so, but otherwise all meetings of boards or committees are limited strictly to members of the committee. To further protect the privacy of the proceedings of a board or committee, its minutes are open to no one except members of the committee.

Procedure in Committee Meetings

The chairman should submit suggested working plans to the committee for consideration at its first meeting. The chairman often discusses plans and a division of duties with committee members even before the first meeting.

Meetings of a committee are called by the chairman. If the chairman fails to act, a meeting may be called by a majority of the members of a committee.

A majority of the members of a committee is a quorum and a majority of the legal votes cast is necessary to take any official action.

Simple and informal procedure is desirable in a committee meeting. Committees follow the ordinary rules of procedure only insofar as they are appropriate to the committee's situation. In committee meetings it is not necessary to stand when making a motion, or to limit the length of speeches, and no seconds are required.

Motions must be accurately stated, discussion confined to the motion or subject, and only one person permitted to speak at a time. In large committees considering controversial subjects, it may be necessary at times to be as formal and to apply parliamentary rules as strictly as in the assembly itself. Most committees find it helpful to keep minutes for the information and convenience of their members.

Committee Hearings

A committee hearing is a meeting during which a committee listens to the viewpoints of members and sometimes of experts on the subject assigned to it. At the end of the hearing the committee, with only its members present, agrees on the conclusions and recommendations that it will present to the membership for their guidance in making the final decision.

Most committee hearings are open to all members of the organization. However, hearings for the purpose of considering matters of discipline, finance, or other subjects that should be decided without publicity that might be harmful to the organization or to a member are open only to members of the committee assigned to conduct the hearing.

The Board of Directors

Few organizations have time in their meetings for the members to plan, discuss, and decide all the matters necessary to carry on the work of the organization. Consequently, the members provide in the bylaws that a small elected group acting as the representatives of all the members shall carry on the work of the organization during the intervals between meetings of the membership. The group is called the board of directors, executive board, board of trustees, or by some other name meaning the governing board.

A governing board is generally composed of the elected officers of the organization, who are members ex officio, and of directors elected by the membership. Usually the president and secretary of the parent body are the chairman and secretary of the governing board. All members of the governing board are sometimes referred to as officers, but the term "officers," as used in this book, does not include the members elected to the board.

The duties, responsibilities, and powers of the board of directors should be clearly defined in the bylaws. Such a board is usually delegated the duty and power of acting for the membership in the intervals between meetings, except that certain powers are vested exclusively in the members and that the membership can overrule the board. The final authority of any organization remains in its "members assembled." Any action of a governing board can be rescinded or modified by the membership, except when the matter has been specifically delegated to the board in the bylaws or when the matter acted on no longer remains within the control of the organization. The board also has specific duties and responsibilities assigned to it.

All members of a governing board share in a joint and collective authority which exists and can be exercised only when the group is in session. Members of a board have no greater authority than any other member of the organization except when the board is meeting. Officers and members to whom specific duties are assigned perform the duties of their office or assignment in addition to sharing in the group authority and duties of the board.

Business transacted at a board meeting should not be discussed except with other directors, unless and until the information has been issued to all members or to the public by the proper authority. The minutes of a board are open only to its members, because the board considers many matters that cannot be discussed outside of the board without injury to the organization or to its members.

Most organizations give continuity to the board by staggering the dates of election of members to the board so that there are always experienced members on the board.

The Executive Committee of the Board

Since many boards cannot meet on short notice, it is customary to provide for a small executive committee of the governing board. A board of directors has the inherent power to appoint an executive committee from its own membership. This committee, usually made up of the president and two or three other officers, is delegated the power to act for the board, with limitations, when it is not meeting.

The specific powers and duties of this committee should be provided for in the bylaws. Some organizations give the executive committee extensive power to act for the board. Others limit it to acting on emergency matters or on recurring matters that must be disposed of promptly.

An executive committee reports to the board at its next meeting or by mail, and its actions are reviewed and included in the minutes of the board.

Conflicts of Interest

A director or officer of an organization may have business dealings with the organization, except when prohibited by the bylaws or by statutory law, which is not common. The officer has both a legal and moral duty, however, to disclose any interest in such a transaction, and must deal fairly, avoiding any transaction not in the best interests of the organization.

Tax-exempt status of an organization is another reason for caution in dealings between the organization and a member of its governing board. If a transaction is found to unduly favor a director or officer, the tax-exempt status of the organization under the Internal Revenue Code may be jeopardized.

Chapter 21

COMMITTEE REPORTS
AND RECOMMENDATIONS

Form of Committee
Reports and Recommendations

Committee reports usually include:

1. A statement of the question, subject, or work assigned to the committee, and any important instructions given to it

2. A brief explanation of how the committee carried out its work

3. A description of the work that the committee performed or, in the case of a deliberative or investigating committee, its findings and conclusions

A committee report should be as brief as possible, consistent with clarity. It should give the background necessary to an understanding of any recommendations the committee is making for decision by the assembly. Credit is given to anyone rendering unusual or outstanding service to the committee, but the report does not give special mention to those who only perform their expected duties.

Recommendations from the committee should be attached to the report but should not be included in it. Each recommendation should be in the form of a motion or resolution to be presented, discussed, and acted on as a separate motion by the voting body. If opinions and recommendations are included in a report, and the report is approved, they are binding on the organization. Such a blanket commitment is dangerous.

Agreement on Committee Reports

The report and the recommendations of a committee must be agreed on at a meeting of the committee. The committee members must have the opportunity to hear all the different viewpoints on the questions involved and to discuss them freely with each other. Otherwise, the report cannot state the collective judgment of the committee. The approval of a committee report or recommendation by members of the committee individually and separately, without a meeting, is not valid approval unless specifically authorized by the body creating the committee.

When it is difficult or impossible for the members of a committee to meet, the bylaws or a motion may authorize the committee to agree on a report without a meeting. A report may be prepared by the chairman and submitted by mail to the members for their suggestions and approval. Every member of the committee must have the opportunity to review the proposed report and to present objections or changes. Members who approve, sign the report and the recommendations and, if a majority sign, the report becomes the report of the committee.

When a report in its final form has been considered and approved by a majority vote at a committee meeting, it is signed by the chairman and the members who agree with it if they wish to do so. A member may withdraw approval of a report at any time before it is presented. A member who agrees to a committee report with exceptions or reservations may indicate the portions with which he or she does not agree and sign the report, signifying approval of the remainder.

Presentation of Committee Reports

At the time in the order of business for committee reports, the presiding officer calls for each report in turn. Standing committees usually report first in the order in which they are listed in the bylaws and are followed by special committees in the order of their appointment. The order of presenting reports, however, should be flexible to meet the needs of the particular meeting, and the order of presentation may be varied by majority vote or by general consent. A committee report is presented by its chairman or by some member of the committee designated to report. The reporting member may introduce the report with a brief explanation if necessary. If a committee report is long, usually only a summary of it is presented orally.

In conventions or annual meetings of large organizations, committee reports usually are printed in advance and distributed to members by mail or at the convention. In this case, the committee chairman makes such explanatory statements as are needed and presents only the recommendations of the committee.

Consideration of Committee Reports

A committee report, after being presented to an assembly, is open for comment, questions, or criticism, but the members of the committee and their motives may not be attacked.

A committee report cannot be amended except by the committee, since no one can make the committee say anything it does not wish to say. A committee report, after it is presented, may be disposed of in any of the following ways:

1. The report may be filed. This is the usual method for disposing of a committee report. It may be filed automatically or ordered filed by a motion, or the presiding officer may announce, "The report will be filed," and proceed to the next item of business. A report that is filed is not binding on the assembly but is available for information and may be considered again at any time. An expression of thanks to the committee may be combined with a motion to file the report.

2. A subject and the report covering it may be referred back to the committee if further study, modifications, or recommendations are needed.

3. Consideration of a committee report may be postponed definitely to a more convenient time.

4. A report may be adopted. This commits the assembly to all the findings and opinions contained in the report and to any recommendations that might be included in it, but not to any recommendations submitted separately. A committee report can be adopted in part or with exceptions or reservations. The word "accept" is sometimes used instead of adopt, but the word "adopt," which cannot be misunderstood, is preferable. A motion "to receive" a committee report is meaningless, since an organization cannot refuse to receive and hear the report of its authorized committee. Since the adoption of a committee report binds the assembly to everything in the report, organizations are wise to file reports instead of adopting them.

5. A final or annual financial report from a treasurer or finance committee is referred to the auditors by the presiding officer without a motion. No final financial report is adopted without an accompanying report from the auditors certifying its correctness.

6. If a financial report concerns proposed or future expenditures only, as in a budget, it is treated as any other financial recommendation of a committee.

Record of Committee Reports

After a committee report has been presented, the reporting member hands it to the secretary for filing in a special book or file reserved for committee reports. A committee report is not included in the minutes unless the assembly votes that a brief summary be included.

Reports of standing committees are usually filed in chronological order under the name of each committee. Reports of special committees are usually filed in alphabetical order according to the subject or name of the committee.

The minutes of each meeting should state what reports were presented, by whom, and the disposition of each report and should record the page or file number where the particular report may be found.

Minority Reports

If any members of a committee disagree with the report submitted by a majority of the committee members, they may submit a minority report signed by members who agree to it. More than one minority report may be submitted. A minority report can be presented only immediately after the majority report. A minority has the right to present and read a report, even though a motion is pending to dispose of the majority report. However, if a motion to dispose of the majority report is pending, the minority report is not voted on, unless a motion is made to substitute it for the majority report. If such a motion to substitute is adopted, the assembly is committed to the recommendations of the minority report, and the majority report is filed for reference. If the motion to substitute fails, the minority report is filed for reference.

Presentation of Committee Recommendations

Recommendations may be acted on separately when they are presented with the committee report, postponed to a definite time, or taken up under new business. When several recommendations are interrelated and have not been printed or sent to the members previously, they should all be read before considering and voting on the individual recommendations.

Whenever the assembly desires to consider the recommendations, the chairman of the committee reads the first recommendation of the committee and moves its adoption.

The motion should be stated in a form that will allow the assembly to vote directly on the proposal itself, not on whether to agree or disagree with the recommendation of the committee. For example, if a committee recommends "that a membership drive should be held in the spring of each year," the motion should be stated to the assembly as "I move that a membership drive be held in the spring of each year." This statement of the proposal allows the assembly to consider, to apply motions (for example, the motion to amend), and to vote directly on the actual proposal. This motion is much clearer than a motion such as "I move that we concur with (adopt, reject, accept, approve, or agree with) the recommendation of the committee."

A well-stated motion requiring a decision directly on the proposal prevents the confusion caused by such motions as, "I move that we approve the recommendation of the finance committee rejecting the proposal of the treasurer to modify the system of keeping financial records." It is impossible to amend or affect this motion in any way that will reach the original proposal, even though the members may wish to do so. The original motion should be stated: "I move that the treasurer be authorized to modify the present system of keeping financial records." The presiding officer or the chairman of the committee would then state for the information of the members that the original motion had been proposed by the treasurer and that the finance committee recommends a "no" vote on it.

After a motion embodying a recommendation has been stated to the assembly, it is considered and acted on as any other main motion.

Chapter 22

CONVENTIONS AND THEIR COMMITTEES

General Structure of Conventions

A *convention* of an organization is the series of consecutive meetings when members and delegates assemble to transact important business, consider developments in the organization's particular field, exchange ideas and experiences, and enjoy the fellowship of others who share a common interest.

Every member of an organization is entitled to attend the convention, but in most organizations the voting on issues is done by the delegates or by a smaller elected legislative body such as a house of delegates. In most international, national, and state conventions, reports and certain general issues are brought before a voting body composed of the elected delegates of the various constituent and component groups, affiliates, chapters, or branches of the parent body. Usually these larger organizations provide that most of the enormous volume of business shall be transacted by a smaller legislative body.

Instruction of Delegates

Voting delegates to a convention may be instructed, partially instructed, or uninstructed by the group they represent. Usually the local groups meet and talk over issues to be voted on by their delegates at the convention. Thus the delegate becomes familiar with the opinions of the group he or she represents.

Except in unusual circumstances, it is not wise to give delegates explicit instructions as to how they must vote. If the delegate were simply a messenger carrying a vote, it would be more economical simply to send the vote by mail.

At a convention a delegate learns new facts and listens to the arguments of others from different localities and with differing viewpoints; frequently a proposal is changed so completely by amendments adopted at the convention that it is really a different proposal from that originally offered. For these reasons a delegate usually should be free to weigh the pros and cons and vote according to what appears to be the wisest course, instead of being required to follow blindly the instructions of a constituency which may be unaware of the full range of arguments pro and con, and of the final wording of the resolution or motion.

The first duty of a delegate is to vote for what the delegate believes is best for the organization as a whole; the second duty is to vote for what is best for the particular constituency represented. The delegate is first a legislator for the whole organization and second a representative of a particular group. A delegate should understand thoroughly how constituency members feel about the proposals to be voted on but should be trusted to exercise good judgment in voting on measures as they are finally presented for decision.

Convention Committees

Committees common to most conventions are the credentials, rules, bylaws, and program committees. Many larger organizations also have some form of reference or resolutions committee.

The *credentials* committee must report before any item of business is presented to the voting body, so that it is known which members are entitled to vote and how many members make up the voting body. This committee examines the credentials of each member or delegate, authorizes the issuance of the badge or card admitting members to meetings, and prepares a list of the members who are entitled to vote.

At the first business meeting the credentials committee gives a preliminary report listing the delegates, alternates, and members who make up the various classes of membership in attendance at the convention. As soon as this report has been adopted by the convention, it becomes the official list of delegates and members of the convention and determines the voting strength (number of members eligible to vote) of the convention. Supplementary reports are usually given daily as new members or delegates present their credentials and are certified by the credentials committee. A final report is given at the concluding business meeting.

The *rules* committee usually submits its report after that of the credentials committee. Since the rules ordinarily vary only slightly from one convention to the next, the report of the rules committee listing the proposed rules frequently is published and distributed to members beforehand.

Convention rules are adopted by a majority vote and can be suspended by the same vote. They ordinarily cover such subjects as seating of delegates and alternates, length of speeches, and privileges of nonvoting members.

The committee on *bylaws* receives and reviews amendments to the bylaws sent in by members or by constituent groups, and usually may propose amendments of its own. The committee makes recommendations, if it wishes, approving or disapproving each proposed amendment and giving the reasons for its decision. The committee can revise or combine several similar amendments, with the permission of their proposers. The committee cannot kill any proposed amendment by failing to report it to the voting body. If the committee were given the power to decide which amendments should be presented to the voting body and which should be withheld, it would have the power to control amendments to the bylaws.

The *program* committee of a convention is responsible for planning the schedule of meetings, activities, and special events of the convention. The committee should work closely with the organization's president, and with other committees. Its plans are submitted to the convention for approval, at which time they become the order of business of the convention. Once the order of business has been adopted it is no longer under control of the program committee, and any subsequent changes must be made by the convention itself. Minor changes in program are usually approved by general consent.

Use of Reference (or Resolutions) Committees

The reference committees of various organizations differ in details, but their purposes and methods are fundamentally the same. The duty of a reference committee is to screen main motions that are to come before the convention, except for those which previously have been screened by some other committee. A reference or resolutions committee also is usually responsible for preparation of courtesy resolutions to be submitted to the assembly, such as those thanking speakers or outgoing officers, etc.

The reference committee holds a hearing on each proposal assigned to it, at which time any member may speak. It also investigates each proposal as needed, and recommends to the voting body what action should be taken on it.

This is necessary because there is not time during most conventions for delegates to consider proposals sufficiently to vote intelligently; nor is there always time to hear all delegates wishing to speak on particular proposals nor for all important business to be transacted. Reference committees can solve all of these problems. By dividing the work of hearing, investigating, and making recommendations on proposals among a number of small representative groups, the organization provides opportunities not only for delegates but also for other members to present their views on proposals. Also the voting body is able to transact an enormous amount of business with a thorough understanding of the facts about each proposal.

Reference committees are usually appointed by the presiding officer of the voting body. Each reference committee should be representative and is usually composed of from three to seven respected members experienced in the committee's particular field.

Most organizations require that all proposals for consideration by the voting body be submitted by a certain date in advance of the convention. Special provision is made for emergency proposals to be submitted during the convention. Proposals in the form of motions or resolutions usually may be submitted by constituent or component groups, or committees or boards of the organization and in some groups by individual members. Recommendations from standing or special committees and proposed amendments to the bylaws or policies are also referred to appropriate reference committees. Some organizations also refer all reports of officers and committees to reference committees for study, evaluation, and comment.

In larger organizations each reference committee has a general field of work, such as finance or service to members. In smaller organizations all proposals usually are divided among three or four general reference committees. In some small organizations, the regular standing committees serve as reference committees at their convention.

As soon as possible after the opening of the convention each delegate is given a list of all the proposals submitted, including the name of the reference committee to which each proposal has been referred, and the time and place of the hearing on it.

Hearings must be scheduled with care to ensure that the more important proposals in a particular field or in related fields are not set for the same time. Members interested in several proposals should be able to attend hearings on each.

If a proposal comes within the field of interest of more than one reference committee, it may be referred to several reference committees. Each reference committee holds hearings and reports on the proposal from the viewpoint of its particular field of interest, or several committees may hold a joint hearing. When there is a joint hearing, each committee usually submits its own recommendations to the voting body.

Duties of Reference Committees

The primary duty of a reference committee is to recommend to the voting body an appropriate course of action on each proposal that has been referred to the committee. This duty requires that a committee hold a hearing open to all members interested in a particular proposal.

The committee then should evaluate each proposal referred to it; consider all relevant comments or recommendations on it that are sent to it by the board of directors, the board of trustees, the bylaws committee, or other groups of the organization; weigh all statements made during the hearing; obtain as much available information and advice as possible; and recommend the best course of action to be taken by the voting body on the proposal.

A reference committee must make a recommendation to the voting body on each proposal assigned to it. The committee may not "pigeonhole" or fail to return a proposal for any reason; the voting body must receive the proposal and dispose of it.

Hearings of Reference Committees

During a hearing the members of a committee usually are seated at a table in the front of the room. They listen to comments and opinions of all members. The committee members may ask questions to be sure that they understand the opinions being expressed, or may answer questions if a member seeks clarification; however, the committee members cannot enter into arguments with speakers or express opinions during the hearing. The committee listens carefully and evaluates all opinions presented so that it may provide the voting body with a carefully considered recommendation.

The chairman of the reference committee presides at the hearings and facilitates discussion. As far as possible all who wish to speak should be heard and a few persons should not be permitted to monopolize the discussion. The committee may limit the length of time assigned to each speaker. The chairman cannot permit motions or votes at the hearing, since its objective is only to receive information and opinions; decisions of any sort during the hearing would hamper the reference committee in its private deliberations.

After the hearing, the committee holds a meeting with only its members present to discuss and evaluate the proposals and opinions expressed by the members and to vote on its recommendation to the voting body. A minority recommendation may also be submitted.

Reports of Reference Committees

Reference committees may call on officers, staff members, or experts in order to gain as much information as possible on which to base their recommendations. A reference committee may recommend amendments to proposals that have been referred to it and may submit proposals of its own. It may make an explanation of the reasons for the committee's decision before offering its recommendations. It may recommend that a proposal be adopted, rejected, amended, or otherwise disposed of.

The recommendation of the reference committee is usually a deciding factor in determining the decision of the voting body. The great influence exercised by the committee, however, is advisory, and it is important that every voting body have the opportunity to consider all proposals submitted to it and to make the final decision on them.

Chapter 23

MINUTES

Importance of Minutes

Accurate, concise, and complete minutes are of vital importance to an organization. They are the official history and legal record of the proposals, reports, and decisions of the members. Minutes are invaluable for reference, and the courts give them great weight as evidence. Auditors depend on them for proof of authorization for important expenditures.

Responsibility for Minutes

The elected secretary working under the direction of the president is responsible for taking notes on all actions at business meetings, preparing minutes from these notes, reading the minutes to the assembly, recording any corrections, and certifying the minutes by signing them when they have been approved by the organization. If a verbatim record is taken, or if the meeting was tape-recorded, the secretary uses such sources as an aid in preparing the official minutes, but is responsible for the completeness and accuracy of the minutes. This responsibility cannot be delegated.

The members of an organization or board are responsible for pointing out errors and approving the minutes.

The secretary is the official custodian of the minutes. The minutes of an organization are open to inspection by members at any reasonable time. Minutes of a board or committee meeting are available only to members of the board or committee.

Preparing Minutes

The secretary should prepare the minutes as soon after a meeting as possible, and should sign them, which indicates a belief that they are an accurate record of the proceedings of the meeting. Ensuring the accuracy of the minutes is a duty the secretary cannot delegate. An employee may prepare the minutes under the secretary's direction, but cannot sign them.

Reading and Correction of Minutes

The presiding officer calls on the secretary to read the minutes at the proper place in the order of business. The reading of the minutes may be postponed for the current meeting by a motion to this effect. However, organizations should not make a practice of postponing the reading of minutes since delay makes it more difficult for members to detect errors. Until the minutes are approved by the assembly they are not official, and they should not be approved until they have been either heard or seen either by the assembly or by a designated committee.

After the secretary has read the minutes, the presiding officer asks, "Are there any corrections to the minutes?" When corrections are suggested, they are usually approved by general consent. The presiding officer may say, "If there is no objection, the error pointed out by Mr. A will be corrected."

If there is disagreement on a proposed correction, the presiding officer, without waiting for a motion, may take a vote to decide whether the correction should be made.

The secretary makes minor corrections in ink immediately and initials each one. Any substantial correction is made as an appendix to the minutes that are being corrected. A reference to the appended correction is inserted at the place to which the correction applies. The statement of the corrections is recorded as approved actions of the body in the minutes of the meeting at which the corrections were made. If an error in the minutes is discovered at a later time, the error may be corrected by the assembly regardless of the lapse of time. The correction and final approval of the minutes are the duty of the assembly.

If the organization has a standing committee on minutes, this committee usually corrects the minutes and reports to the organization at regular intervals. On the certification of the minutes committee that the minutes are correct, the body may approve the minutes by general consent or by majority vote.

After the minutes have been entered in the minute book, no corrections except in spelling or punctuation may be made unless they have been approved by the assembly.

Some organizations send copies of minutes to members after each meeting in order that members may study them and be prepared to bring up any corrections at the next meeting.

Approval of Minutes

If there are no corrections—or after all corrections have been made—some member may move to approve the minutes as read, or as corrected, or the presiding officer may take a vote on their approval, or may state: "If there are no further corrections, the minutes are approved as corrected."

Before the assembly has approved the minutes, they are merely the secretary's record. When the minutes have been approved, and the secretary has certified them as the official approved minutes by writing the word "Approved" at the end of the minutes, entering the date, and signing them, they become the *official* minutes of the organization. Some organizations require that the president also sign, and some direct the president and the secretary to initial each page of the minutes.

What Minutes Should Contain

Minutes vary greatly according to the needs of different organizations. In general, minutes are a record of all actions and proceedings but not a record of discussion. The opening sentences must record the date, hour, and place at which the meeting was called to order, the type of meeting (regular, special, or continued), the name of the presiding officer, and the fact that a quorum was present. The minutes of a special meeting should also include a copy of the notice or call for the meeting.

The minutes record all motions or resolutions, whether passed or lost, with the name of the proposer, and the way in which each motion was disposed of. The exact wording of all motions should be recorded. It is not sufficient to state that a motion "was amended and finally adopted." When a vote is taken by division which is counted, or by ballot, the number voting on each side is recorded. The record of each member's vote on a roll call is entered in the minutes. No member can have views or protests on a motion recorded in the minutes unless a motion permitting such action is passed by majority vote.

Each report should be recorded with the name of the member presenting it, the action taken on the report, and reference to the file where the report may be found. An important report is sometimes summarized briefly in the minutes and the file reference given for the complete report. The statements of business transacted should be specific. A statement such as "letters were read" or "reports were given" is of no value. Each letter read should be identified or summarized briefly and the action on it, if any, recorded.

Minutes of committees are often kept by the chairman, but in large committees a secretary may be appointed. Committee minutes are generally brief, but in some cases they may be more detailed than those of meetings of the organization because they often serve as the basis for the committee's report. Minutes of committee hearings frequently list persons who speak for or against proposals and often summarize the facts presented by each speaker.

What Minutes Should Not Contain

The secretary's personal opinions, interpretations, or comments should not be included in the minutes. Descriptive or judgmental phrases, such as "an able report" or "a heated discussion," have no place in a factual record of business.

Adverse criticism of members should never be included except in the form of a motion censoring or reprimanding a member. Praise of members should appear only in the form of officially adopted votes of thanks, gratitude, or commendation.

The Minute Book

An exact copy of the official, approved minutes should be entered in a suitable record book and kept in a safe place. If a loose-leaf book is used, the minutes should be bound at the end of each year. An index to each year's minutes by subject, date, and page is useful. It is also important to keep in the minute book copies of the charter, bylaws, rules, policies, and procedures of the organization for quick reference in meetings. (See *Model Minutes,* Appendix C.)

Chapter 24

CHARTERS, BYLAWS, AND RULES

Types of Charters

An organization looks to the law as its highest source of guidance on procedure and to its charters and bylaws as the next-ranking sources. Charters are of two types—charters of incorporation from government and charters from a parent organization. Many organizations hold charters of both types. The charter from government ranks above the charter from a parent organization.

The charter of an incorporated organization is a grant, usually by a state government, to a group of persons of the right to incorporate and to operate for specific purposes under the laws governing profit or nonprofit corporations. In some states this charter is termed the *articles of incorporation.* The charter of a nonprofit corporation usually contains its name and business address, a statement of the purposes of the organization, and provisions for members, a governing board, and officers.

The charter should provide for its own amendment by the membership, subject to the approval of the governmental body that issued the charter. No amendment to the charter or articles of incorporation is effective until it has been approved by the membership and also by the governmental authority that granted the charter. Amendments to charters are adopted by the same rules and procedures as amendments to the bylaws.

The charter from a parent organization is a certificate issued to a group of persons giving them the right to operate as a subsidiary unit of the parent organization. The regional organization holding the charter is subject to the provisions in the charter or bylaws of the parent organization that relate to its constituent and component organizations.

Constitution and Bylaws

Some organizations adopt both a constitution and bylaws. The constitution establishes the fundamental framework of the organization, and to amend it usually requires a higher vote than does amendment of the bylaws. The bylaws supplement these fundamental provisions and are easier to amend.

Most organizations combine the provisions of a constitution and bylaws in one document called bylaws. A single document is more practical because all provisions relating to one subject are in one place.

Drafting Bylaws

Good bylaws alone do not make an effective organization; they are an outline of its structure. However, suitable bylaws are necessary to enable an organization to function well.

Bylaws should be concise and are best arranged in outline form. Many organizations keep their bylaws simple and brief by including only essential provisions and supplementing them with adopted procedures.

The best bylaws are those which are written to meet the needs of the particular organization. A provision that works well for one organization may be entirely unsuitable for another. Bylaws should be custom-made to fit each individual organization.

Adoption of the Original Bylaws

When the presiding officer calls for the report of the committee appointed to draft the bylaws, the committee chairman first moves the adoption of the proposed bylaws in order to bring them before the assembly for consideration and discussion. The presiding officer states the motion, "It has been moved and seconded that the bylaws be adopted. The chairman will read the first section."

The chairman reads the first section of the first article and the presiding officer calls for discussion, questions, or amendments to it. If an amendment to the section is proposed, the presiding officer states it to the assembly and after discussion it is voted on, but only amendments, not articles or sections, are voted on at this time. The presiding officer then calls for the reading of the next section and follows the same procedure. When the reading and amendment of all the bylaws are completed, the presiding officer asks, "Are there any further amendments to the bylaws? Is there any further question or discussion?"

When all proposed amendments have been voted on and when no one rises to discuss the bylaws further, the presiding officer takes the vote on the motion to adopt the bylaws. A majority vote only is required for their adoption.

When Bylaws Go into Effect

The bylaws go into effect immediately with the announcement of the vote adopting them unless the motion to adopt provides that the bylaws, or some portion or provision in them, is not effective until a later date. For example: "I move that the bylaws be adopted as amended, with the reservation that Article IX, Section 4, that provides for regular monthly meetings, will not go into effect until January 1 of next year."

When a good set of bylaws has been drafted and adopted, an organization should try not to clutter them with unimportant amendments. The bylaws committee should strive to give the new bylaws a chance to be tested thoroughly before proposing amendments. Amendments, unless vital, should be withheld until a number of changes can be made at one time, or until a revision is needed. Important constructive work is often neglected at annual meetings and conventions because so much time is devoted to unimportant amendments to the bylaws, rules, or procedures.

Provisions for Amending Bylaws

It is good practice for an organization to include in its bylaws specific requirements covering the following:

1. How and by whom amendments to bylaws may be initiated and proposed

2. The form in which proposed amendments should be stated

3. The date before which proposed amendments must be received by the organization

4. The required notice to members of proposed amendments

5. The vote required to adopt the amendment

Proposing Amendments to Bylaws

In many local groups, any member may rise while new business is being considered and offer an amendment to the bylaws simply by stating the proposed amendment and giving a copy of it to the secretary. In most groups the amendment is then referred to the bylaws committee, which studies it and reports the recommendation of the committee to the voting body. The bylaws of most organizations require prior notice for bylaws amendments, in addition to either a two-thirds vote or a vote of a majority of the entire membership, and many have a standing rule or a custom that bylaws changes must be reviewed by a committee. Some groups also limit consideration of bylaws amendments to the annual meeting.

State, national, and international groups ordinarily require that amendments be proposed by constituent or component groups or by a committee or a board of the parent organization. These organizations require that proposed amendments be sent to the bylaws committee by a certain date preceding the convention. The bylaws committee usually considers and makes recommendations on each amendment. The proposed amendments are published with the committee's recommendations on them; also included are notice of the date and time that the amendments are to be considered and voted on, and notice of any hearings to be held on them. (See *Notice of Proposed Actions,* p. 99.)

Form for Proposed Amendments to Bylaws

Unless the bylaws provide differently, a proposed amendment should be stated in such language that, if adopted, it may be incorporated directly into the bylaws and should be sent in this form as a notice to all members.

The following is a simple method of stating a proposed amendment:

Amendment I. *Proposed Amendment to Article VI, Section 1 of the Bylaws.*

"To Amend *Article VI, Board of Directors, Section 1, Membership,* by striking out the words 'three members elected by the House of Delegates' and inserting in their place the words 'five members elected by the Assembly.'

"If *amended,* the section will read: *Section 1, Membership,* 'The Board of Directors consists of the President, Vice President, Secretary, Treasurer, Immediate Past President, and five members elected by the Assembly.'"

Considering Amendments to Bylaws

At a meeting or convention, when the time arrives for considering the proposed amendments, the chairman or some other member of the bylaws committee reads the first proposed amendment as it is stated in the notice and moves its adoption. Since a proposed amendment to the bylaws is a main motion, it may be amended, and amendments to that amendment are also in order. These amendments to the proposed amendment require no previous notice and require only a majority vote for their approval, even though the proposed motion to amend the bylaws may require previous notice and a higher vote.

When the required notice has been given concerning a proposed amendment to the bylaws, the law holds that the subject covered by the amendment has been opened to change and gives the assembly wide discretion in amending the proposed amendment. Parliamentary law, however, provides that:

1. The proposed amendment must be germane to the section to which it applies

2. No amendments can be proposed that cannot reasonably be implied by the notice given on the proposed amendment to the bylaws

If an organization wishes to restrict further the extent or type of amendments to proposed amendments to the bylaws, it must include provisions for the additional restrictions in the bylaws.

Since notice of the proposed amendment to the bylaws has been given, the members are aware that the particular amendment and the subject that it covers will be open to amendment without further notice at the meeting. For example, if a proposed amendment to a section of the bylaws entitled *Classes of Membership* adds a new provision establishing an additional type of membership—associate membership—members know that the proposed amendment may itself be amended by providing or changing the qualifications, rights, or privileges of the proposed class of associate members. Amendments pertaining to other classes of membership are not in order, since notice does not state or imply amendments to any class of membership except associate membership.

An amendment to another part of the bylaws not specified in the notice is admissible only if it is reasonably implied by the amendment as stated in the notice. Using the same example, if the original amendment provided for the creation of an associate membership class, the necessity of fixing the dues for associate members would reasonably be implied, although the subject of dues is covered in another part of the bylaws and might have been omitted unintentionally in the proposed amendment. An amendment providing the dues for associate members would therefore be admissible.

If a provision in a proposed amendment conflicts with a provision already in the bylaws, the conflicting provision in the bylaws can also be amended to conform to the newly adopted amendment without additional notice.

Vote Required on Amendments to Bylaws

The vote required to amend the bylaws should be stated in the bylaws. Because the adoption of the original bylaws requires only a majority of the legal votes cast, some organizations consider it logical to permit amendment with the same majority vote, provided there was advance notice of the proposed amendment. It is more common, however, to require either a two-thirds vote, with prior notice, or a majority vote of the entire membership.

Revision of Bylaws

After bylaws have served for a considerable period of time, it may be necessary to amend many portions of them. The simplest method, when extensive changes are required, is to select a special committee for this purpose or instruct the bylaws committee to study the bylaws and submit a revision. The report of a special revisions committee or of a bylaws committee is a revision when it proposes a substantial number of changes that may affect considerably the structure of the organization, or a rewriting of the form of the bylaws for clarity or reorganization.

A copy of the proposed revision with notice of the date when it will be considered and voted on should be sent to each member in advance of the meeting or convention. Any necessary explanation should be inserted before the provision to which it applies. A revision proposes, in effect, a new set of bylaws, and the revision is presented, considered, and voted on under the same procedures as those followed for the adoption of the original bylaws. The original bylaws, which are still in effect, are not before the assembly for consideration. A revised set of bylaws requires only a majority vote for adoption.

A revised set of bylaws automatically becomes effective immediately after the vote adopting the new revision. It is possible, however, to provide in the motion to adopt the revised bylaws that certain portions of them should not become effective until a later specified time.

Interpreting Bylaws and Rules

Organizations frequently have difficulty in agreeing on the interpretation of their own bylaws and rules. It is wise to assign the duty of interpreting the bylaws and rules to the committee on bylaws or to the board of directors. The interpreting group may seek the advice of an attorney or a parliamentarian.

Special and Standing Rules

Organizations sometimes adopt rules of procedure that add to or vary from the rules of parliamentary law as stated in their parliamentary authority. The rules that are temporary and intended to meet a current or special situation are termed *special* rules. The rules that are intended to stand until revoked are termed *standing* rules. Organizations have the right to adopt special or standing rules by majority vote without notice and to abolish or amend them in the same manner.

Parliamentary Authority

The rules and procedures contained in the parliamentary authority adopted by an organization are intended to cover all parliamentary situations not otherwise provided for in the law or the charters, bylaws, or other rules adopted by an organization.

The adopted parliamentary authority is provided for in the bylaws. This provision is best stated as follows: "The current edition of *The Standard Code of Parliamentary Procedure* governs this organization in all parliamentary situations that are not provided for in the law or in its charter, bylaws, or adopted rules."

Detailed Procedures

There are many minor details of procedure that are necessary to carry out the provisions of the charter, bylaws, and adopted rules. These detailed procedures should not be included in the bylaws as they will add length and confusion. These procedures adopted by an organization are called *adopted procedures*. They are changed more frequently than the bylaws or more important rules and require only a majority vote to adopt or to change. They should be classified under suitable headings, for example, "Procedures of Election Committee."

Supplementing Procedural Rules by Motions

An organization has the inherent power to take any action that is not in conflict with law, its charter, bylaws, or adopted rules. This includes the power to adopt motions regulating the conduct of its current business. Since many situations arise that are not covered by rules, it is essential that the details of transacting business be determined by motions. During the course of proceedings, motions are frequently necessary to facilitate the method, manner, or order of transacting business.

For example, if a committee has submitted five recommendations relating to the same subject, and the chairman has moved that the first recommendation be adopted and it is being considered, some member might move that the fifth recommendation be considered and decided first because it states a general policy on which the other four recommendations depend.

The power of an organization to adopt any motions for the conduct of current business is particularly important during elections. For example, when there are several candidates for an office and no candidate receives the required majority vote, it is often impractical to require that successive votes be taken until one candidate receives the necessary majority vote. An organization has the power to adopt motions to enable it to complete the election within a reasonable time. Organizations sometimes vote, for example, to drop the candidate having the lowest vote from the list of candidates, after each successive vote. Or an organization may decide to reopen nominations for the office in order to secure a candidate on whom a majority can agree. Organizations have wide leeway in adopting motions to determine the conduct of pending business.

Adopted Policies

Bylaws define the structure of an organization. Policies define the beliefs and philosophy. Both are equally binding on the organization. Organizations frequently adopt policies that are as important in determining the action of the group as are its bylaws or other rules. Policies are usually formulated to meet recurring problems that come up for decision. Most successful businesses have written policies that have developed from experience and that guide their operations. Many organizations develop policies that have an equally powerful influence on their effectiveness.

Once a policy has been developed and adopted, it sets a standard for judging and deciding all new proposals dealing with the subject or situations covered by the policy. If a proposal is contrary to an adopted policy of the organization, it is not in order and is not considered.

Organizations that use policies as guiding principles should provide in their bylaws for their adoption, vote required, and the method for amending and reviewing them. Some organizations review their policies each year to see whether changes or new policies are required. Many organizations provide for a standing committee on policies which maintains a list of currently effective policies, considers and makes recommendations on proposed policies, reviews all policies annually, and interprets them when requested.

Policies should not be included in the bylaws but should be compiled separately and stated appropriately. The following are examples of policies:

1. "This association believes that because its fundamental purpose is to educate, its programs should always include speakers representing both sides of any controversial or political subject and that equal time should be given each speaker."

2. "We adhere to a policy or raising our professional standards by strict screening of applicants for membership. The professional character of our organization can best be advanced by gradually increasing, but never lowering, the eligibility requirements of applicants for membership."

3. "This organization believes that current services to members is its most important function. Our policy is that dues should not be saved, accumulated, or invested for future use, but that all revenue from dues should be used to provide a constantly improving and expanding current program of services to our members."

4. "This organization adheres strictly to the policy that no member may give gifts or gratuities to any employee of the organization."

Chapter 25

FINANCES

Setting Up Financial Records

Every organization, large or small, should establish and maintain an appropriate accounting system for its funds. A good system for controlling finances saves time and money. Therefore, it is wise for even a small organization to consult an accountant when it is establishing or revising its financial records.

Report of the Treasurer

At each regular meeting the treasurer should give a brief report or summary of the collections and expenditures and call attention to any unusual items. The presiding officer should then inquire whether there are any questions about the treasurer's report.

The treasurer should make a complete report annually. All members should receive copies of this report, the auditor's certification, and any recommendations made by the treasurer or auditor.

If an organization has a finance committee, it should report at least annually, giving a realistic picture of the financial situation and problems of the organization and of any contemplated proposals or plans involving finances.

Report of the Auditor

Organizations should have an audit at least once a year. An auditing committee composed of members is helpful but is not the best financial safeguard of the organization's finances. Better results can be obtained if the members of the committee are trained in keeping financial records.

The auditor should be selected by vote of the governing board or membership. The treasurer and staff members concerned with finances should have no voice or part in selecting the auditor or the type of audit.

Certified and licensed public accountants are authorized by law to express professional independent opinions on the financial statements of an organization. They may also be requested to provide comments on important financial expenditures, methods, and safeguards and on the integrity of the accounting system and practices.

An auditor's report is an opinion on the treasurer's report. There are two main types of report that auditors provide:

1. The standard *short-form* report consists of two paragraphs expressing the auditor's opinion on the financial statements. The short-form report usually is adequate for most organizations. The standard form, if no exceptions are indicated, means that in the auditor's opinion the treasurer's report reflects fairly the current financial condition and results of operations of the organization, in conformity with generally accepted accounting principles applied on a basis consistent with that of the preceding year. If an exception is expressed in the opinion, the reasons for the exception should be carefully investigated.

2. The *long-form* report, in addition to the contents of the short-form report, describes and explains in detail the significant items in the financial statements. It may also include further explanations of the audit procedures performed by the auditor. The long-form report is more expensive and most organizations consider it unnecessary unless the board of directors or the management of the organization need detailed financial information that is not otherwise available.

Financial Safeguards

Among the financial safeguards set up by some organizations are: The adoption of a budget; the requirement of authorization for purchases; strict supervision of officers, committees, or employees who collect or expend funds or incur financial obligations; an annual audit; and a blanket bond covering all members and employees who have access to organization funds.

Most organizations prepare and adopt a budget of estimated collections and expenditures. A budget is an estimate only. Adoption of a budget does not mean that the organization must observe its provisions unless required to do so by the rules of the organization. More often, the budget is a financial guide. Some groups require the authorization of the governing board or the membership for any expenditure in excess of the amount provided for in the budget. They also provide that any expenditure not included in the budget requires the same authorization.

A few organizations provide that proposed expenditures above a nominal amount require a purchase order or some other form of authorization and that unusual and particularly large expenditures require authorization by vote of the board of directors or of the membership.

Only members and employees specifically authorized should be permitted to commit the organization to an expenditure. If an authorized representative purchases goods or services in the name of the organization, the bill must be paid by the organization regardless of whether the members later vote to pay or not to pay it.

Instructions to any committee should state how much money, if any, the committee is authorized to spend. Unless a committee is authorized to collect, hold, or expend funds, all funds should be collected, held, and expended through the regular financial channels of the organization.

Chapter 26

LEGAL CLASSIFICATIONS
OF ORGANIZATIONS

Meeting to Form an Organization

Since it is difficult for a large assembly to formulate plans, a small group or committee of founders should meet to consider and come to decisions on such questions as the purposes of the proposed organization, its legal form (temporary or permanent, profit or nonprofit, incorporated or unincorporated), types of membership, financing, policies, temporary officers, and affiliation with other organizations.

At the organizing meeting (sometimes referred to as a "mass meeting") one of the group calls the meeting to order and nominates or calls for nominations for a temporary chairman. If additional persons are nominated, a vote is taken on each until one candidate receives a majority vote. This nominee is then declared the temporary presiding officer, and calls for nominations for a temporary secretary who is elected in the same manner. The presiding officer then requests a member of the group to explain the purpose of the proposed organization. Someone may then present a motion or resolution for forming the organization.

A resolution for forming a *temporary* organization might read:

"*Resolved,* That this assembly form a temporary organization, to be known as the Waterfront Preservation Committee, for the purpose of protesting against the action of the County Board of Supervisors in authorizing a freeway along the waterfront; and be it further

"*Resolved,* That a committee attend the next meeting of the County Board of Supervisors to present a signed protest against this freeway; and be it further

206

"*Resolved,* That a copy of this resolution with the reasons for our opposition and a list of our officers be sent
to each newspaper in this county."

A motion to form a *permanent* organization might read:

"I move that we organize as the Sharon Civic Association."

If this motion carries, some member moves to appoint a committee to draft bylaws; or if the bylaws have already been prepared, they are presented. As soon as the bylaws have been
adopted, permanent officers are elected and the organization is
complete. (See *Adoption of the Original Bylaws,* p. 194.)

If the members decide to seek a charter as a unit of an
already-existing organization, they select or authorize the presiding officer to appoint a committee to carry out this procedure.

Temporary and Permanent Organizations

An organization may be established as either a temporary or a
permanent organization. A temporary organization may exist for
a few meetings or even a single meeting. It dissolves automatically as soon as the members accomplish the purpose for which
they organized. An example of a temporary organization is an
organization to elect a candidate to office.

A permanent organization is one formed with the intention
of functioning over a considerable period of time, indefinitely,
in perpetuity, or until it is dissolved.

Incorporated and
Unincorporated Organizations

The founders of a new organization or the members of an older
organization who wish to reorganize must decide whether they
wish to incorporate or to remain unincorporated. Those nonprofit, unincorporated organizations that are rather loosely struc-
tured and operated only under a set of their own rules are
termed *associations.* These associations are sharply limited with
regard to tax exemption, property holding, and gift-receiving
powers. Most organizations, whether local, state, national, or in-

ternational in scope, are incorporated. The chief advantages of incorporation are:

1. The organization holds a charter from government. Usually this is granted by the state in which the organization incorporated. It operates under the guidance and protection of the state laws governing corporations.

2. The purposes of the organization and the powers necessary to carry out these purposes have legal recognition.

3. The individuals or member groups are able to work with greater effectiveness and scope by joining their resources and efforts.

4. The organization exists permanently until dissolved, even though its membership changes.

5. The corporation is recognized as a legal entity apart from its individual members and thus can do business and hold property of any kind in its own right.

6. Officers, directors, and members are free from personal liability for debts of the organization.

7. The name and seal of the organization are legally protected.

Statutory Requirements

If a nonprofit association is incorporated, members should be aware that in addition to having their bylaws and practices comply with their corporate charter (sometimes called "articles of incorporation") they also must comply with state corporation codes. Many of these codes set specific guidelines for such things as quorum requirements, election procedures, notice required for meetings, etc. An attorney should be consulted when a corporation is set up, to ensure that the charter and bylaws conform to state statutes and to federal and state requirements for tax-exempt status.

Most state corporation codes do not, however, provide detailed guidance on the conduct of meetings. They permit the organization to adopt its own parliamentary authority or code of procedure, such as this book, and to establish its own bylaws and rules so long as these do not conflict with the corporate charter or with statutory or common law.

Labor unions also should be aware that their bylaws must conform to provisions of federal law, particularly the Labor-Management Reporting and Disclosure Act of 1959, better known as the Landrum-Griffin Act. On procedural matters not covered by the act, the union should be guided by the basic principles of common parliamentary law, and should adopt a parliamentary authority to resolve questions not dealt with in the act or in the union's bylaws.

Nonprofit Organizations

Almost all voluntary organizations are nonprofit groups. The first requirement of a nonprofit corporation is that its purposes be ethical, social, moral, or educational. The activities of a nonprofit organization may be charitable, political, social, governmental, or educational in character. The second requirement is that any income or profit of the organization must be used solely to carry out its legal purposes and cannot be distributed as profit to its members. The organization cannot pay dividends or other remuneration to its members. It can, however, pay reasonable compensation or salaries for services rendered.

A nonprofit organization may receive profit incidental to its operations, but that profit must be used for the purposes for which the organization exists. For example, a state medical association having tax exemption as a nonprofit organization might receive considerable profit from some of its activities; this money could not be distributed as pecuniary gain to its members, but it could be expended for educational or other purposes that would benefit its members and the public.

A nonprofit organization, whether incorporated or not, may apply to both the federal and state government for tax-exempt status.

Chapter 27

RIGHTS OF MEMBERS AND OF ORGANIZATIONS

Relationship Between Member and Organization

Upon joining an organization, a member enters into an implicit contract with the organization. No particular procedure is necessary to establish this relationship so long as a mutual understanding as to membership is reached. Some organizations require members to sign the bylaws or go through an initiation ceremony, whereas others provide that an applicant becomes a member the moment application for membership is approved, upon payment of dues and initiation fees, if any.

A person who joins an organization accepts the organization as it then is. The charter, bylaws, and other rules of the organization as they then exist are a part of the contract binding both the member and the organization.

However, the rights of members do not necessarily remain unchanged. Privileges of members may be taken away by decision of the voting body, or other privileges may be added. Fees and dues can be changed, and assessments levied if provided for in the bylaws, but vested rights, those that have been acquired as a result of the contract between the member and the organization, cannot be taken away.

All changes in the rights and privileges of members and all changes in the rules of the organization must be made according to the provisions for making such changes contained in the bylaws or parliamentary law.

Rights of Members

In addition to the rights a member has as a person, there are also associational rights, property rights, and parliamentary rights, all of which are protected by law. A member's associational rights stem from membership in the organization. For example, a member has the right to fair and equitable treatment from the other members of the organization.

Property rights also may be involved with membership in the organization, such as an interest in a clubhouse or other assets owned by the group.

A member also has the following fundamental rights under common parliamentary law, subject only to any specific limitations contained in the bylaws:

1. To be sent notices

2. To attend meetings

3. To present motions

4. To speak on debatable questions

5. To vote

6. To nominate

7. To be a candidate for office

8. To inspect official records of the organization

9. To insist on the enforcement of the rules of the organization and of parliamentary law

10. To resign from an office or from the organization itself

11. To have a fair hearing before expulsion or other penalties are applied

12. To receive or have the right to inspect an up-to-date copy of the bylaws, charter, rules, and minutes of the organization

13. To exercise any other rights or privileges given to the members by the law, by the bylaws, or by the rules of the organization

The rights of membership may vary depending on whether the person is a regular member, an associate member, a life member, or some other type of member.

If any of the associational, property, or parliamentary rights of a member are violated, legal action may be taken against the organization. As a general rule, however, courts will not adjudicate such actions until the member has exhausted the means provided for enforcing such rights under the rules of parliamentary procedure and the bylaws of the organization.

Rights of Organizations

An organization itself has rights. These rights are exercised by the decision of a majority of its members. Some of the fundamental rights of an organization are:

1. To carry out its purposes and to exercise any of the rights or authority granted it by law

2. To change its purposes, if permitted by law and its charter, to merge with another organization, or to dissolve

3. To establish eligibility requirements and procedures governing the admission of members, and to grant or refuse membership according to the law and its adopted rules

4. To establish and to amend, through changes in its bylaws, the rights, privileges, and obligations of its members either by extension or limitation

5. To delegate authority, within legal limits, to officers, boards, committees, and employees

6. To select its officers, directors, and committee members and to suspend or remove them for valid cause

7. To discipline or expel members in accordance with the law and with its bylaws

8. To hold property and to defend or enter into litigation in its own name if it is incorporated

Relationship of Individual and Organizational Rights

The rights of each member are definite and are protected by law; they must, however, be regarded in relation to the rights of the other members and of the organization. In order to assert the rights of membership, the member must choose the proper time and must follow the proper procedure. For example, a member has the right to present any proposal to the assembly. But this right cannot be exercised at a special meeting by proposing a motion that is not stated in the call for the special meeting.

Similarly, a member has the fundamental right to be heard on any debatable question before the assembly. However, if the member attempts to discuss the question when it has not yet been presented, or for a second time when others desire to speak, or when some other member has the floor, or after debate has been terminated by a motion to vote immediately, the right to discuss does not apply.

If the rights of an individual member or a minority of members conflict with the rights of the majority of the assembly, the rights of the majority ultimately must prevail. For example, a minority has the right to be heard. But if the minority attempts to be heard when a majority wishes to adjourn, its right must give way to that of the majority.

The right of members to oppose ideas and candidates does not extend to the right to undermine the organization itself. If after the majority has made a decision some members continue to oppose to the point where the organization has difficulty in functioning or is in danger of being destroyed, the governing board or the membership should protect the organization by taking proper disciplinary action.

Discipline and Expulsion of Members

Procedures for the discipline and expulsion of members should be included in the bylaws. However, every organization has the inherent right to discipline, suspend, or expel a member for valid cause, even if provisions for doing so are not included in the bylaws.

Discipline may consist, for example, of requiring a member to appear before the governing board and explain certain actions or pay a fine, or a member may be reprimanded or suspended from membership for a limited time.

A membership can be terminated and a member expelled because of violation of an important duty to the organization, a breach of a fundamental rule or principle of the organization, or for any violation stated in the bylaws as a ground for expulsion. In general, termination of membership is justified if a member fails or refuses to work within the framework of the organization.

In addition, an organization has the implied power to expel a member for violation of duties as a citizen. For example, a member may be expelled upon conviction of a criminal offense that would discredit the organization.

A proceeding to expel a member must not violate any rule of the organization or any of the member's rights under the law. The primary requisites for expulsion proceedings are due notice and fair hearing.

The essential steps for imposing severe discipline or expelling a member are:

1. *Charges.* Charges in affidavit form stating the alleged violations and preliminary proof should be filed with the secretary.

2. *Investigation.* The proper committee should investigate the charges promptly and, if it decides that a hearing is warranted, set a date and notify the secretary.

3. *Notification.* The secretary should send the accused member a registered letter at least fifteen days before the date of the hearing, containing a copy of the charges, the time and place of the hearing, and a statement of the member's right to be present at the hearing, to present a defense, to be represented by an attorney, and to receive a copy of any transcript.

4. *Hearing.* In conducting the hearing the committee should preserve decorum and fair play, restrict evidence and testimony to the written charges, and uphold the right of the accused member to present a defense, to cross-examine witnesses, and to refute the charges which have been made.

5. *Decision.* The hearing committee should within a reasonable time make findings of fact on the essential points at issue, recommend a decision of guilt or innocence, and send a copy of the recommended decision and findings of fact to the accused member and to the secretary.

6. *Penalty.* If the member is found guilty of the charges, the board of directors should recommend a penalty to the membership meeting. The decision may be approved by a majority vote of the legal votes cast at the meeting.

Some organizations permit a member who has been expelled to apply for readmission after a certain period of time.

Resignations

A member has the right to resign from an organization at any time. A provision in the bylaws that a member's dues must be paid up before the member resigns cannot prevent a resignation. There is no practical way in which an ordinary society can compel a delinquent member to continue as a member, nor can it persist in assessing and collecting dues. An exception to this rule would be when property ownership involves agreement to maintain membership in an organization, as in the case of a condominium association.

A resignation becomes effective immediately, unless some future time is specified by the resigning member, and no acceptance of it is necessary to make it effective.

An officer or director may resign from office at any time. A resignation need not be written, and it may be implied, as when a member moves out of the jurisdiction of the organization and is no longer eligible for membership. A bylaws provision that an officer shall hold office "until a successor is elected" does not prevent the officer from resigning, nor can it be used to force a person to remain in office.

A resignation effective at some future date may be withdrawn until it has been accepted, or until the effective date of the resignation; if, however, the resignation is intended to become effective immediately, it cannot be withdrawn.

An officer or director who has resigned either orally or in writing cannot simply resume office because of a change of mind. A person who has resigned from office can be restored to that office only by reelection, if it was an elective office, or by reappointment, if it was an appointive office. After resigning, an officer or director continues to be liable for acts committed or concurred in before resignation.

Chapter 28

STAFF AND CONSULTANTS

The Executive Secretary

Most large organizations and many local groups employ a chief administrator who is variously called executive secretary, executive director, or manager. The person is chosen by the governing board and is responsible to the board.

This administrator needs an extensive knowledge of planning for and administering voluntary organizations, and experience with business methods, as well as the ability to adapt to a constantly changing group of employers. The executive secretary should have the skill and the willingness to assist officers, committees, and members. An executive secretary is usually most effective when working quietly behind the scenes, avoiding the limelight and letting the elected officers get credit and appreciation. A good executive secretary will stand aloof from the politics and rivalries of members, working for the overall good of the organization.

The executive secretary directs the administration of the organization, employs staff members with the approval of the governing board, and performs any other duties assigned by the voting body, the governing board, or the president.

A competent and loyal executive secretary is a great asset to any organization, providing continuity within an association whose leaders are changing frequently and whose members are busy with their own occupations.

The Accountant

An organization that handles any considerable amount of money will find that an accountant can save the organization time and money by establishing or revising its accounting system to meet the particular needs of the group. The accountant may audit the financial records and prepare tax reports, and can comment on the significance of various items in the auditing report.

The Consultant
to Nonprofit Organizations

Nonprofit corporations and organizations are concerned with professional, educational, or political objectives, and often work almost entirely with unpaid volunteers; therefore they often require the services of consultants who are experienced in working with such groups.

A good consultant to nonprofit organizations, in addition to understanding parliamentary procedure, must have a working knowledge of financial procedures, communication techniques, tax exemption, and principles of sound organizational management.

The Attorney

An organization needs the help of an attorney on all important legal matters. Situations in which an attorney's services are essential include:

1. Decision on the type of organizational structure that legally is best suited to the purposes of a new organization; for example, association, society, nonprofit corporation, profit corporation, or a type of foundation

2. Incorporating the organization

3. Establishing a foundation for the organization

4. Entering into or altering an important contract

5. Transactions involving the purchase, lease, or sale of real property or important personal property

6. The merger or the dissolution of the organization

7. Expulsion of a member

8. Initiation or defense of litigation

The Parliamentarian

A competent parliamentarian can be helpful to any organization, and in large organizations a parliamentarian's services are essential to effective operation.

The parliamentarian is usually chosen by the president and works under the direction of the president. The parliamentarian also aids and advises the governing board, committees, members, and staff members. In most large organizations the parliamentarian is retained on an annual basis, and therefore is available at any time for assistance to members who need advance consultation in planning for a meeting or convention. After the meeting the parliamentarian can advise on problems that arise in carrying out the decisions of the membership.

At a meeting or convention the parliamentarian usually sits next to the president. The parliamentarian cannot make rulings, but advises the presiding officer, who does make rulings. If a question is asked, the parliamentarian will explain the answer to the president only, or, if the president directs, may reply so that all the members may hear. At the request of the presiding officer the parliamentarian may explain a procedure to the members. If a serious mistake is being made, the parliamentarian unobtrusively calls it to the attention of the presiding officer, who then decides what action to take.

The more capable and experienced a presiding officer is, the better he or she understands the value of a good parliamentarian. The experienced presiding officer understands that a parliamentarian can assume responsibility for keeping track of procedural problems and details, so that the presiding officer is free to concentrate on the overall progress and tone of the meeting. This enables the presiding officer to proceed with confidence and poise.

The parliamentarian is not an advocate of causes or a representative of any group within the organization, but is retained to help the members do what they wish to do and to find a valid way of accomplishing, if possible, the legitimate purposes of the organization.

Many parliamentary problems involve several rules and principles. A parliamentarian must be able to reconcile the conflicting principles and rules of parliamentary law that may be involved in a particular situation. When asked a question the parliamentarian must give a considered opinion as to how the rules and principles apply. Having been retained as an authority, the parliamentarian should neither argue nor seek to prove the correctness of an opinion by quoting from books, any more than a doctor would cite a medical authority in explaining a diagnosis to a patient. Having given an opinion, the parliamentarian explains it only if there is a need to do so.

Chapter 29

DEALING WITH DISAPPROVED
OR OBSOLETE MOTIONS

To conform to modern usage and theory, several troublesome motions reflecting nineteenth century customs have been omitted from this book, and some archaic and misleading terms have been supplanted by more understandable language. Old practices die hard, however, and the user of modern procedures occasionally will encounter motions or terminology not recommended in the *The Standard Code*. This chapter is intended to provide guidance in such cases.

Adjourning to an Adjourned Meeting

Traditionally the word "adjourn" has been used for two opposite meanings: an adjourned meeting could be either one which had ended or one which had reconvened after an adjournment; the resumed meeting was sometimes referred to as an " adjournment" of the original meeting. To avoid confusion it is recommended that the resumption of a meeting which was temporarily adjourned be referred to as a "continued" meeting.

Call for the Orders of the Day

Older usage had a special privileged motion, a call for the orders of the day, to be used whenever some matter was not taken up at the scheduled time.

Instead of using this quaint phrase, which is usually puzzling to many in the audience, a member might say, "Madam President, I request that we take up the matter which is scheduled on the agenda for this time." In effect, this is a point of order, and thus gives the member the right to interrupt, if necessary. (If preferred, the member may state the request formally as a point of order.)

Committee of the Whole

The Committee of the Whole is a procedure under which the assembly pretends it is a large committee, in order to get around limitations on debate. Although generally obsolete except in legislative bodies, it is still proposed sometimes in other organizations.

The procedure requires that the presiding officer turn the chair over to a temporary "committee chairman," and discussion continues with some alteration in limits on debate. All votes are only "committee votes," not binding on the assembly, so they must be taken over again after the committee has resolved itself back into an assembly with the original presiding officer again in the chair, and after the committee chairman has "reported" to the assembly on what the committee did. The absurdity of this procedure has caused the practice to fall into disuse in recent decades, though it is still found in some of the older parliamentary manuals.

If someone moves that "the assembly resolve itself into a committee of the whole," the presiding officer should explain that the same purpose can be achieved by a motion to consider informally (see p. 120).

Dispense with the Reading
of the Minutes

This phrase should be avoided because it means different things to different people. If the intent is to *postpone* the reading of the minutes, the motion should include that word to avoid misunderstanding, and preferably should indicate when the reading is postponed to. If the intent is to approve a *written* version of the minutes which has been distributed, the motion should be "to approve the minutes as distributed." If the intent is to submit the minutes to a *committee* for approval, the motion should say so. If the intent is to certify that the minutes are correct without giving anyone a chance either to hear or read them, however, the motion is out of order (see *"Dispensing" with Reading of Minutes,* p. 110).

When a member moves to dispense with the reading of the

minutes, the chair should determine the intent, and either re-state the motion or rule it out of order.

Fix the Time to Which to Adjourn

Some parliamentary manuals give the highest precedence to a privileged motion to fix the time to which to adjourn, a motion for which there is really no need.

If an unqualified motion to adjourn is made when there is no provision for a further meeting, the motion is, in effect, a motion to dissolve the assembly. It is a main motion, subject to an amendment specifying a time for a continuation of the meeting. The presiding officer should explain that the assembly may, if desired, amend the motion so that it becomes a motion to adjourn to a continued meeting.

Object to Consideration

Some of the older parliamentary manuals provided that a member could "object to consideration" of a motion before discussion had begun. This would require that the chair call for a vote on whether the motion should be considered, and consideration could be prevented by a two-thirds vote in the negative.

The motion was rarely used, and when it was it often caused consternation for the inexperienced presiding officer, who was unfamiliar with the term and was unaccustomed to requiring a two-thirds vote in the *negative* (a requirement that applies to no other motion).

There are simpler ways to prevent discussion of a question. When it is desirable to avoid considering a matter, usually there is a good reason: necessary facts aren't available, or a key person is not present, or it could be handled better in committee, or there isn't time in the current meeting, or the motion is unnecessary, or it is outside the scope of the bylaws, or proper advance notice was not given, or the motion is frivolous or dilatory, or it is out of order for some other reason. In such cases the simplest procedure is a brief explanation followed by a motion to postpone temporarily, to postpone to a specified time, to refer the matter to committee, to request to the maker that the motion be withdrawn, or to raise a point of order.

If the motion doesn't fall into any of these categories—if it is desired to avoid any discussion of the motion simply because consideration might be embarrassing to some member or guest, or to the organization itself, or for any other reason, a member can move to table the motion. If this is done *before any discussion*, it is the equivalent of objecting to consideration, and in such a case the motion to table requires a two-thirds vote.

Although killing a motion by tabling is frowned upon in some of the older parliamentary manuals it has been a common practice in American usage for more than a century. As long as it is done by a two-thirds vote in situations where it prevents any discussion from taking place, it provides the same protection as did the awkward procedure of objecting to consideration.

Postpone Indefinitely

The motion to postpone indefinitely was often confused with the motion to table, because they both set aside the pending main motion without bringing it to a direct vote. Unlike to table, however, postpone indefinitely was debatable, and also opened the main question to debate. Because theoretically it was a new motion, it provided a loophole for those who had exhausted their right of debate, enabling them to get around the limitation and continue debating the main motion. This practice has been criticized because it prolongs debate, and because it violates the principle of majority rule, providing a means of thwarting the will of the assembly as expressed in the motion limiting debate. It also confuses those who are not familiar with the motion, and who assume that it would merely "postpone" the pending question, as the name might seem to indicate, instead of killing it.

The motion to lay on the table, or, as it is more commonly called, the motion to table, accomplishes the main purpose of the motion to postpone indefinitely—that is, it suppresses the main motion without bringing it to a direct vote—but without the unintended result of prolonging discussion without the assembly's permission.

Legislative bodies have traditionally killed motions by tabling them, and this is the most common method of "postponing indefinitely" in American organizations of all kinds. It is recommended that when a motion is made to postpone indefinitely, the chair handle it as a motion to table.

The Previous Question

To the person unfamiliar with parliamentary procedure nothing is more perplexing than the use of the phrase, "I move the previous question," to end discussion and bring a question to a vote. Keeping in mind that in almost every assembly there are a few such people, the chair should make sure that all members understand that they are voting not on the pending motion, nor on the "previous" motion, but on *whether to close debate and vote immediately* on the pending motion. This is unnecessary, of course, when the maker uses the more modern terminology: "I move to close debate."

When the maker of the motion uses the term "previous question" instead of moving to close debate, the chair should explain, "The previous question has been moved and seconded. If passed, this motion would require that we close debate and vote immediately on the pending motion. All in favor of closing debate please rise..." etc.

Quasi-Committee of the Whole

The Quasi-Committee of the Whole is a variation of the Committee of the Whole, the chief difference being that the presiding officer remains in the chair instead of appointing someone else as temporary chairman. The procedure is equally confusing. When the motion is proposed, the chair should explain that the procedure is not used under *The Standard Code of Parliamentary Procedure,* and (with the maker's permission) should treat the motion as a motion to consider informally.

Reconsider and Enter on the Minutes

This variation of the motion to reconsider permitted two members of an assembly (one to make the motion and one to second it) to thwart the will of the majority. Because this violates the most basic rule of democratic procedure it is not permitted under *The Standard Code of Parliamentary Procedure,* although it is still found in some parliamentary manuals.

The purpose of the motion was to force reconsideration of a vote which had just been taken—but with a stipulation that the reconsideration would be delayed until the subsequent meeting, and that the minutes of the current meeting would indicate that notice had been given of intent to call up the motion to reconsider at the next meeting. The mere making of this motion had the effect of nullifying, temporarily, the decision of the assembly, the rationale being that since the matter was going to be reconsidered it was still "pending," no matter how overwhelming the vote by which it had been passed. The motion has been called the "monkey-wrench motion," because in effect it throws a monkey wrench into the smoothly operating machinery of majority rule, and there is no easy way of countering it.*

When this motion is made it should be ruled out of order. The chair should explain, however, that at a subsequent meeting the motion that was just passed may be rescinded; or if the motion was defeated it may be reintroduced. In the meantime, however, the vote stands as the decision of the assembly.

Simplification of Motion to Reconsider

Under *The Standard Code,* the motion to reconsider can be applied only to the main motion. For all other motions renewal can be achieved by simpler and more direct means.

When a motion is made to reconsider the vote on a procedural question, the chair should declare the motion out of order, and should explain to the maker what alternative is available. (See *When Can a Motion be Renewed?,* p. 28.)

---

*One way of coping with abuse of this motion was suggested by General Henry M. Robert, who said in *Robert's Rules of Order Revised* (p. 167), "Should a minority make an improper use of this form of the motion to reconsider by applying it to a vote which required action before the next regular business meeting, the remedy is at once to vote that when the assembly adjourns it adjourns to meet on another day, appointing a suitable day, when the reconsideration could be called up and disposed of." It is doubtful, however, that many modern organizations would approve of calling a special meeting for the sole purpose of dealing with a parliamentary maneuver.

Chapter 30

OFTEN-ASKED QUESTIONS

The questions that follow are among those most frequently asked in seminars on parliamentary procedure. Most of them are discussed elsewhere in more detail, but for quick reference they are included here as a separate section.

When an organization's bylaws disagree with its parliamentary authority, which should it follow?

Its bylaws. A parliamentary authority, such as this book, is intended as a backup, to apply in situations not covered by bylaws or standing rules.

If an organization has followed certain practices for a long time, are these practices considered rules of the organization?

Yes. Custom and tradition can establish unwritten rules which are valid, provided they do not conflict with bylaws.[1] To avoid misunderstanding, however, it is advisable to put them in writing as standing rules.

Is it really necessary to follow parliamentary procedure in a meeting? Isn't it easier to conduct business informally?

Informality is often very desirable—and parliamentary procedure permits great informality when appropriate.

The need for formal procedure varies with the size of the group. A committee of three or four people obviously doesn't need elaborate rules governing its procedure, and members may even be allowed to interrupt each other, so long as basic courtesy is being observed. In a committee of ten or twelve, much greater control must be exercised by the chair. And in a meeting of thirty or forty people, it is impossible to proceed in an orderly fashion and protect essential rights without adherence to predetermined rules of procedure.

It also should be remembered that some actions are not legal unless done correctly. Such matters as the proper calling of the meeting, the presence of a quorum, and correct voting procedures can determine the validity of what is done at a meeting.

Parliamentary procedure is flexible enough to be useful in all circumstances. For example, if an assembly wishes to discuss a matter at length before formulating a motion, this can be accomplished by passage of the motion to consider informally.

What can the presiding officer do to prevent strife within an organization?

Hostility within organizations usually results from what is perceived as unfair treatment. People who believe their motion was defeated because the majority disagreed with them are disappointed, but seldom hostile. Hostility occurs when members believe (rightly or wrongly) that they lost because the chair favored the other side, or because they were not allowed to present their case fully, or because proper procedures were not followed.

The presiding officer therefore should always make sure that an unpopular viewpoint is given a fair hearing. To "gavel through" a proposal by refusing to recognize opponents who want to speak builds resentment and plants the seeds of future discord. It also is an abuse of the power of the chair. If it becomes necessary to end discussion when a determined minority wants to continue, the presiding officer should make sure that the action is taken not by the chair, but by the assembly, with a two-thirds vote on a properly proposed motion to close debate.

Another cause of bitterness is when discussion becomes personal, and members are allowed to comment on the motives, competence, or character of other members. It is the duty of the presiding officer to stifle such behavior immediately by ruling it out of order. Failure to do so may result in the development of a full-blown personal feud, which can plague an organization for years to come.

When several members are seeking the floor, how does the chair determine which one to recognize?

When a motion has been made, the maker of the motion should be recognized first, if he or she seeks the floor, to explain the reasons for the motion. From that point on, the first person to stand and address the chair generally should be recognized.

When several members seek recognition, however, the chair should give preference to one who has not spoken previously, and an effort should be made to balance the discussion, rather than permitting several consecutive speeches on the same side of the question.

Can a member stand during another person's remarks, in order to be sure of being the first person to address the chair when the speaker is through?

No. Members should remain seated while someone else has the floor. This rule should be enforced by the presiding officer.

What are the essential differences in presiding over an assembly and presiding at a committee meeting?

In an assembly the chair remains neutral on controversial matters, avoiding participation in debate, and refraining from making motions. A committee chairman plays a more participatory role, being free to make motions and to join freely in discussion, while at the same time making sure that both sides are treated fairly.

To use a sports analogy, in an assembly the role of the presiding officer is somewhat comparable to that of a referee. The committee chairman's role is closer to that of a team captain.

What are the main differences in procedure in a committee and an assembly?

In a committee, discussion is generally informal and unrestricted. Members address each other directly, instead of through the chair. Members raise their hands to obtain recognition, instead of standing, and they need not stand when speaking. In a committee or in a board meeting motions do not require a second.

Probably the most important difference between assemblies and committees, however, is that in an assembly one can speak only to a motion that has been made and seconded. In a committee the procedure is usually reversed: a matter may be discussed at great length before a specific proposal is even formulated.

Why is there this difference?

If unchanneled discussion is permitted in a large group people tend to go off in different directions; there is no way of focusing attention on specific points or of reaching concrete decisions. In a small committee, however, group pressure keeps loquacious individuals under control.

The ideal way to solve any problem is to get agreement on precisely what the problem is before considering remedies for it. This is easily done in a committee. In a large, unwieldy assembly, however, this process is often so time-consuming that it is impractical.

Should a board of directors operate as an assembly or a committee?

It depends on size. A small board, such as one of five members, will operate much like a committee. A large board, with perhaps ten or twelve members, should be conducted with much more formality.

Is it possible to explain a motion before making it?

Yes—very briefly. The general rule in an assembly is that all remarks must relate to the pending motion, but prior to making a motion a member may explain in a sentence or two the reason for doing so. Detailed discussion, however, should be deferred until the motion has been made, seconded, and stated by the chair.

What is general consent?

General consent is a way of saving time by avoiding votes on routine or noncontroversial matters. It can be used only when there is unanimous agreement, and is sometimes referred to as "unanimous consent." When it is used the chair always must ask whether there is any objection; if there is, a formal vote must be taken.

For example, if a time limit has been set on speeches and a member requests an additional two minutes to complete an explanation, an experienced presiding officer usually will not call for a formal vote on the request, but will just say, "If there is no objection the speaker may have an additional two minutes."

It is important to recognize, however, that the chair does not have the power simply to grant such a request. By using the phrase, "if there is no objection"—which has been referred to as the "magic phrase," because it permits almost any action to be taken—the chair is acknowledging the right of the assembly to make the decision. If any member objects, general consent does not exist and it becomes necessary to submit the question to the assembly for a vote.

If a quorum is not present for a meeting, what can be done?

A meeting legally cannot be held without a quorum, so there is little the members can do except to remain for informal discussion.

Sometimes an emergency requires that some action be taken despite the absence of a quorum. Those approving such action should realize that risk is involved: the organization is not bound by their decisions, and those who take such actions are individually responsible for them. Emergency actions taken in the absence of a quorum should be ratified later at a properly constituted meeting, in order to remove any doubt as to their validity.

Suppose a quorum was present when a meeting started but has drifted away. Does this invalidate actions taken when a quorum was no longer present?

No. Unless someone raises the question of whether there is a quorum it is assumed that one continues to be present. The existence of a quorum cannot be questioned at a later date. Any action taken after someone had called attention to the absence of a quorum, however, would be invalid.

In some organizations confusion frequently results when a motion is amended. Why is this, and how can it be avoided?

Most problems with amendments occur when members are allowed to violate the most basic rule of procedure: one thing at a time. While an amendment is pending the chair must not permit *any* discussion of the main motion. Only after the amendment has been considered and voted on is the main motion again opened up to discussion (and, if desired, to further amendment).

Discussion of the main motion while an amendment is pending invariably confuses the assembly as to what is being considered. The chair must tactfully but firmly insist that general discussion be deferred until the amendment has been adopted or rejected.

Some people are confused by the amendment process because it seems to involve an extra vote, which appears unnecessary. Why is this?

When an organization is voting on amendments it is not making decisions on what it is going to do; *it is merely deciding on the wording of the motion which ultimately will be voted on.*

Once all proposed amendments have either been adopted or rejected, the motion is in its final form, and after discussion it must then be put to the assembly for a vote. Some inexperienced presiding officers omit this vote on the motion as amended, which is a serious error since no final action has been taken on the proposal.

When someone moves to amend a motion should the chair check to see if the amendment is acceptable to the maker of the motion?

If the chair has not yet stated the motion it is still considered to be in a formative stage, and the maker may accept or reject any changes which are suggested by other members or by the chair.

Once the motion has been stated, however, and discussion has begun, the motion belongs to the assembly, and it is not necessary to get the approval of the maker of the motion in order to amend it. In practice, however, the chair often can expedite matters by obtaining such approval anyway, if it is a "friendly" amendment, i.e., one which is likely to be accepted by the maker of the original motion, such as a slight change in wording for clarification, or to correct an error. By obtaining such approval in advance the chair increases the likelihood of general consent being obtained. If the maker of the motion disapproves of such an amendment, however, it is not automatically rejected; it must then be submitted to the assembly for approval or rejection.

Can an amendment be amended?

Yes. It is advisable to avoid this procedure if possible, how-ever, because it often confuses those unfamiliar with parliamen-tary procedure. If the proposed secondary amendment is a "friendly amendment," i.e., one which is likely to be acceptable to the maker of the primary amendment and to the assembly, it is better to handle it by general consent, as explained above.

When a secondary amendment is put to the assembly for dis-cussion and vote, it is handled in the same way as a primary amend-ment: discussion is limited to the immediately pending question (in this case, the secondary amendment), with discussion of the main motion and the primary amendment being out of order. After the secondary amendment has been adopted or rejected, discussion is in order on the primary amendment (as amended); and after it has been voted on, discussion is in order on the original main mo-tion (or the main motion as amended).

Does the maker of a motion have a right to withdraw it?

Yes—until it has been stated by the chair. After that it can be withdrawn only with permission of the assembly. In most cas-es, however, this is just a formality, because permission is nearly always granted by general consent.

Can the maker of a motion vote against it?

Of course. The motion may have been changed by amend-ment, or facts may have come to light during discussion which convince the maker that the motion is unwise.

Can the maker of a motion speak against it?

Yes. In the past some parliamentary authorities prohibited this, but obviously it is unfair to deny anyone an opportunity to express an opinion simply because the person initially held a dif-ferent opinion.

How detailed should a treasurer's report be?

This is up to the organization. For most groups meeting weekly, monthly, or quarterly, the oral report at a regular meet-ing should be brief, listing just totals, with mention of major ex-penditures or income. In an oral report amounts are often rounded off to the nearest dollar, if there is no objection, to make them more comprehensible.

The treasurer's *annual* report should be submitted in writing, and should be audited as specified in the organization's bylaws.

How does the chair decide whether to call for a voice vote, a rising vote, a show of hands, a ballot vote, or a roll call vote?

The usual method is a voice vote—"calling for the ayes and noes." To verify an indecisive voice vote, the chair should call for a standing vote (or, if the group is small, a show of hands). If a two-thirds vote is required, a standing vote or show of hands generally is used, because of the difficulty in measuring a two-thirds voice vote. (If the chair senses that the vote is likely to be unanimous or nearly so, however, a voice vote may be used.) A ballot vote is used when required by the bylaws, by a standing rule, or by vote of the assembly. A roll call vote is used mainly in conventions of delegates when required by the bylaws or by decision of the assembly.

Any member may move that a particular method be used for voting. This is an incidental motion; it is not debatable and requires a majority vote.

If a ballot vote is not unanimous, can a motion be made to make the vote unanimous?

No. The essence of a ballot vote is secrecy. A member could oppose this motion only by disclosing personal feelings, so the motion is out of order.

Is the secretary required to keep a record of who seconds a motion?

No. Such information serves no useful purpose, and time is wasted ascertaining and recording the name of the seconder.

What should the presiding officer do if he or she is uncertain how to proceed?

If there is no parliamentarian in the meeting, the best procedure may be to say candidly, "The chair is in doubt as to how this matter should be handled. Does anyone have a suggestion?" Usually someone in the group will be knowledgeable enough to suggest a proper course of action. If conflicting suggestions are offered, the chair can either make a choice or leave the matter to the assembly, taking a vote on the various suggestions.

Another alternative is for the chair simply to take whatever action seems most in accord with common sense and fair play, not being unduly concerned with procedural technicalities. The courts have ruled that failure to observe the "niceties of every parliamentary rule" does not invalidate actions taken by an assembly or board, provided basic principles of fairness were followed.[2] As one court observed, "The important inquiry of the court always is whether the number required by law have agreed on a particular measure.[3]

What is cumulative voting?

It is the "bunching up" of votes for one or more candidates, instead of the casting of single votes for a number of different candidates.

For example, if six board positions are to be filled, and each person can vote for six candidates, a voter might choose instead to cast all six votes for one person. This obviously would make the election of that candidate much more likely, although the voter would thereby forfeit the opportunity to influence the election of other members of the board.

Cumulative voting is not permitted unless specifically authorized in the bylaws.[4]

What is bullet voting?

If cumulative voting is not permitted, a similar result can be obtained by casting a vote for one candidate and not voting for anyone else. This procedure is sometimes called "bullet voting." It is permitted unless prohibited by the bylaws.

Can a committee meet by telephone?

Yes, if a conference call is used, so that all members are on the line at the same time and can hear each other. Individual phone calls to committee members, however, are not considered a proper substitute for a meeting, even though all members are contacted.

How many candidates should a nominating committee nominate for each office?

Unless specified in the bylaws or standing rules, the number is up to the committee. The most common procedure is to submit a single slate—one nominee for each vacancy—with a provision for additional nominations to be made from the floor.

Which term is correct, chairman or chairperson?

Chairman is the traditional form and is used by Congress, most state legislatures, and most associations, but an organization is free to use any term it chooses.[5]

When the president or vice president is presiding over an assembly it is preferable to address him or her as "Mr. President" or "Madam President." To refer to the presiding officer in an official capacity it is proper to use the term "the chair," as in, "Will the chair please repeat the motion?"

In a committee, unless the organization has chosen to use some other form, the person presiding is addressed as "Mr. Chairman" or "Madam Chairman."

What are the mistakes most commonly made by presiding officers?

Among the most common are these:

- Taking unnecessary votes on noncontroversial matters instead of using general consent

- Cutting off discussion arbitrarily instead of permitting the assembly to decide when debate should end

- Refusing to permit the making of a motion with which the chair disagrees

- Failure to remain impartial (or to relinquish the chair) when a controversial matter is being discussed

- Failure to stifle promptly out-of-order remarks, such as nongermane discussion or derogatory comments about another member

- Allowing discussion to become too informal, bypassing the chair, thereby causing the chair to lose control

- Failure to call for a final vote on a motion after it has been amended

- Failure to restate each motion carefully before taking a vote, so that every member understands what is being voted on

- Failure to confirm, after a vote, what has been decided, so that the secretary and the assembly understand clearly what was done

The most common mistake of presiding officers, however, is trying to "play it by ear," conducting a meeting without a thorough understanding of parliamentary procedure. In the words of the noted parliamentarian George Demeter, "It is the duty of the presiding officer to know the rules of parliamentary law and basic parliamentary practice. There is nothing more pitiable than one who is ignorant of parliamentary law trying to preside over an assembly; the more intelligent the assembly, the sadder the spectacle."[6]

What are the mistakes most commonly made by members of an assembly?
The most frequent are:

- Failure to obtain recognition before speaking
- Failure to limit one's remarks to the immediately pending question
- Arguing at a personal level, attacking opponents for their past actions or comments, instead of limiting discussion to the subject itself
- Failure to ask questions when uncertain about what is going on
- Failure to raise a point of order when the presiding officer infringes on the rights of members, as, for example, when discussion is arbitrarily cut off by the chair
- Nitpicking insistence on trivial parliamentary technicalities which prevent an assembly from focusing its attention on the substance of what is being discussed

What are the most common errors secretaries make in keeping minutes?

- Failure to record legally significant facts, such as the name of the organization, the date of the meeting (including the year), the presence of a quorum, the name of the person presiding, and the name of the person serving as secretary
- Failure to record motions that were defeated
- Failure to record votes that should be recorded
- Failure to record motions adopted by general consent
- Failure to record (in minutes of boards and committees) the names of those present
- Failure to record previous notice of matters to be brought up at the next meeting
- Failure to record important points of order
- Failure to record appeals from decision of the chair and action taken on them
- Recording detailed description of the program and entertainment
- Recording in a manner that reflects the opinions of the secretary
- Recording comments made in debate
- Recording a detailed account of all procedural motions
- Recording motions that were withdrawn
- Failure to record the time of adjournment
- Failure to sign the minutes of each meeting
- Failure to initial corrections

What is the meaning of the term, "Robert's Rules"?
It may mean any of three things:

1. It may refer to a book by General Henry M. Robert, *Robert's Rules of Order,* published in 1876 and revised in 1915, which for many years was considered the standard American authority on parliamentary procedure.

2. It may refer to a book by General Robert's daughter-in-law, Sarah Corbin Robert, entitled *Robert's Rules of Order Newly Revised,* first published in 1970. (Despite the similarity in titles, Mrs. Robert's book is completely different from the one by General Robert, although it uses the same terminology and procedures.)

3. The term is often used erroneously in conversation as a synonym for parliamentary procedure, indicating that a meeting is to be conducted with formal motions and voting.

If one commonly attends meetings where **Robert's Rules of Order** *is the prescribed authority, would one find it difficult to change to the* **Standard Code of Parliamentary Procedure?**

Exactly the opposite. Some of the terminology in *Robert's Rules* is now outdated, because the book was based mainly on practices common during the Victorian era. The *Standard Code* is intended to present the principles of procedure in modern terms, reflecting the usage encountered in a typical gathering today.

For example, in any meeting that is open to the general public some people will be puzzled by the archaic term, "previous question," but they understand what is meant when someone moves to "close debate" on the pending motion. They will be confused by use of the term "adjourned meeting" to refer both to a meeting which has ended and one that has resumed; the term "continued meeting" for one which has resumed is less likely to cause confusion. And they are likely to be puzzled when someone "calls for the orders of the day," but they know what is happening if someone simply says, "Mr. President, I ask that we now take up the motion that was scheduled for consideration at this time."

Some technical terms of course must be used for precision; but whenever something can be put in words more likely to be understood by people unfamiliar with parliamentary procedure, it is recommended that this be done.

Is more modern terminology the principal difference between the **Standard Code** *and the older parliamentary authorities?*

No. Another difference is the elimination of a number of seldom-used and troublesome procedures, such as the Committee of the Whole, Quasi-Committee of the Whole, to postpone indefinitely, to object to consideration, and to reconsider and enter on the minutes, all of which cause consternation for both the presiding officer and the members when they are unfamiliar with them, as is the case in most meetings.

In addition, the handling of some motions has been greatly simplified. In *Robert's Rules of Order Newly Revised*, for example, it is recommended that opponents of a motion should vote *for* it under certain circumstances, so that they will be eligible to move to reconsider.[7] But casting an insincere vote strikes many people as devious and dishonest, and the practice often causes misunderstanding and resentment. Furthermore, the requirement that a member announce how he or she voted on the matter to be reconsidered violates the principle of the secret ballot, which is one of the most basic rights of democracy—and the requirement is impossible to enforce, anyway, because there is no way to prove how anyone voted except in the case of a roll call vote. Under the *Standard Code* these problems do not arise, because there is no restriction on who may move to reconsider.

Where can one obtain additional information about parliamentary procedure, such as correspondence courses, periodicals, bibliography, cassette tapes, and information about local organizations of parliamentarians?

Write to the executive director, American Institute of Parliamentarians, P.O. Box 12452, Fort Wayne, Indiana 46863.

Appendix A

GOVERNMENTAL BOARDS, COUNCILS, COMMISSIONS, AND COMMITTEES

Governmental Bodies and
Parliamentary Law

Local, state, and national governmental bodies (except state legislatures and Congress, which have their own systems of specialized rules) operate under the common law of parliamentary procedure. All these bodies, whether primarily legislative, administrative, or quasi-judicial, or whether they combine these functions, must comply with any constitutional, statutory, or charter enactments on procedures that apply to them and must also conduct their business in strict accord with common parliamentary law.

Parliamentary law applies somewhat differently to governmental bodies and to voluntary organizations. The powers of voluntary organizations arise from agreement of the members and can be changed by the members. The powers of governmental organizations do not reside in the members themselves and can be changed only by the authority that established them. The powers of governmental bodies are delegated to them by constitution or statute.

The boards, councils, commissions, and committees of government have an even greater obligation to observe correct parliamentary law than do voluntary organizations. They have a responsibility to the public, and their decisions, more widespread and permanent in effect, have greater impact, both moral and financial.

Every governmental body has an inherent right to regulate its own procedure subject to the provisions of the constitution, statutes, charter, or other controlling authority. Although governmental bodies have the right to adopt special rules governing some of their procedures, none of these adopted rules can conflict with the law or with public policy. For example, when a charter provides that interested citizens shall be heard by the council, the council cannot require instead that objections be submitted in writing. Because of the differing responsibilities and legal status of these public bodies, some parliamentary rules that apply to them differ from common parliamentary law, or are supplementary to it. The principles explained here apply unless a statute or an adopted rule of the body provides differently.

The statutory law that controls the procedure of governmental bodies differs in detail in the various states, counties, cities, and districts. However, there are basic principles and rules that apply only to governmental bodies and that are common to all of them.

This section of the appendix alerts such bodies to the parliamentary principles that apply particularly to them and that the law considers important. It also explains the more important parliamentary principles and rules that differ from or are in addition to the common parliamentary law as applied to voluntary organizations, and as explained in this book. The material presented here is intended only for members of governmental bodies.

Organization of Governmental Bodies

A board, council, commission, or committee of government must organize with a presiding officer and a recording officer before it can undertake any business. Usually such bodies reorganize annually and elect officers periodically as the law provides.

A statute may designate the presiding officer and other officers, as when an elected mayor is the ex-officio presiding officer of a city council. Frequently the law authorizes governmental bodies to elect their own officers from their membership, as when a board of education selects its own president and secretary.

If two or more of these bodies meet together as a *joint body*, they must organize as a joint body and choose a presiding officer and a recording officer. If two or more bodies meet as *separate bodies* holding a *joint meeting*, they do not organize jointly, and they cannot take legal action except as separate bodies.

Notice Requirements

A governmental body must adhere strictly to all statutory, parliamentary, or adopted requirements regarding notice of all regular and special meetings and hearings, and of matters requiring notice, if its actions are to be legal. If notice of any meeting or hearing is intentionally or negligently withheld from a member or from others to whom notice is due, the proceedings of that meeting are invalid. Similarly, if notice of any proposal requiring notice is intentionally or negligently withheld from a member, action taken on the proposal is invalid. Notice of special meetings must state the particular subjects to be discussed and the specific proposals to be voted on.

In certain instances the law requires governmental bodies to give public notice of those meetings and hearings that are open to the public; for example, a budget hearing. Some proposals require notice to persons who have a particular interest in the business to be considered at the meeting or hearing; thus, a board of supervisors must send notice to all property owners within the boundaries of a proposed new improvement district. Many governmental bodies also are required to publish notice of the time and place of their regular meetings. All such requirements regarding notice must be fulfilled if the actions of the body are to be valid.

A defect in notice to members can be overcome only if all the members of the body (or all the persons affected) are present and vote to waive the defect. However, no waiver by the members can validate actions taken at a meeting if the actions are invalid for any other reason.

Quorum

The quorum of governmental bodies is usually fixed by statute or ordinance or by an adopted rule of the body. If it is not thus determined, the rule of common parliamentary law governs and a quorum consists of a majority of the members of the body. (See *Quorum Requirements,* p. 104.) The most common statutory requirement for a quorum is that it consist of a majority of the positions or memberships of the body. This requirement is not changed by vacancies or disqualification of members.

When two or more bodies come together in a joint meeting but do not organize as one joint body, the quorum is a majority of each body computed separately. When two or more bodies meet and organize as one joint body, the quorum is a majority of the members of the joint body.

If there is not a quorum present at the time set for the meeting, the body cannot be called to order; legally, there can be no meeting until a quorum is present. If there is not a quorum, those present cannot fix a time for another meeting. If a special meeting is desired, the procedure for calling such a meeting must be complied with; otherwise, there can be no meeting until the next regular meeting.

If at any time in a meeting a quorum ceases to be present, the presiding officer or some member should immediately raise the question of no quorum, and the question of the presence or absence of a quorum should be determined immediately and recorded in the minutes. If at a later date a question of the lack of a quorum at the time of taking a particular action is raised, the courts will presume that a quorum continued to be present if the minutes show that a quorum had been present previously at the meeting and do not show by a vote, roll call, or statement that a quorum had ceased to be present at the time of taking the particular action. (See *Presumption of a Quorum,* p. 106.)

Minutes

All actions taken by governmental organizations must be fully and accurately recorded in their minutes. The minutes are the primary evidence of actions taken by the body; they determine whether proposals were adopted and state specifically what the proposals were. When ordinances, laws, or rules are printed separately, they may be identified in the minutes by subject, name, and number instead of being included in full.

The final legal responsibility for correcting and approving the minutes rests solely with the members of the body. If the district attorney, for instance, is assigned the duty of correcting the minutes of a board of freeholders, the responsibility for correcting and approving them as the correct and official minutes of the body still rests with the members.

If during a meeting an employee records a verbatim report

from which the minutes are later prepared, the members are still responsible for the accuracy of the minutes, and the secretary whose duty it is to sign them cannot finally attest them until after they have been prepared, corrected, and approved by vote of the body. Only then does this record of actions become the official minutes of the body. An employee may prepare the minutes, but only the secretary of the body may attest them after their approval by the body.

Minutes of governmental organizations, with the exception of closed hearings or meetings to consider such matters as the hiring or dismissal of employees, or sale or purchase of property, are a part of the public record and are available to the public at reasonable times.

Presiding Officer

The presiding officer in a governmental body is usually a member and has all the rights and duties of the other members, including the right to introduce motions or proposals and to speak and vote on them while presiding. Since each member of these bodies often is elected or appointed to represent a segment of opinion or a geographical area, the group represented by the presiding officer would be deprived of representation if the presiding officer did not have the same rights as other members.

Powers and Duties of Members

The powers and duties of most boards, commissions, councils, and committees are joint powers and duties that can be exercised only when the body is meeting. Individual members do not have authority to act individually and independently, because of the fact that they are members of the body. An exception to this principle is when specific duties or powers are assigned by statute or delegated by vote of the body to a certain member or members or to a committee of the body.

The legislative and administrative powers and responsibilities, when vested in such a body, may be exercised only in the meetings of the body.

No member of a governmental body has the right to speak or act for it unless specifically authorized by law or by the body.

Ex officio members of these bodies have the same rights and duties as the other members of the body unless the law provides differently.

A governmental body cannot delegate any discretionary powers or duties to any other persons or groups, not even to a committee of its own members or officers or to its individual members. It can assign ministerial or administrative duties or powers that do not require the exercise of discretion but merely involve the faithful performance of acts. Public bodies are more severely restricted than voluntary organizations in delegating their authority or discretionary power. (See *Delegation of Authority by Officers and Boards,* p. 161.)

No Seconds Required

Seconds to motions, resolutions, or ordinances cannot be required in governmental bodies and no proposal can be ruled out of order for want of a second.

Voting

The vote required on different types of proposals is usually specified by statute. The required vote for most proposals is a majority of the members or memberships of the body. A majority of the memberships means, for example, that a board having twelve positions, two of which are vacant, requires a majority of seven. If there is no statute or adopted rule specifying the vote required, the rule of common parliamentary law governs; that is, decision by the majority of the legal votes cast.

Unlike voluntary organizations, governmental boards, councils, commissions, and committees cannot limit their powers by adopting a rule requiring more than a majority vote to pass an ordinance, or enactment, or a nonprocedural motion. Any requirement in excess of a majority vote to take such actions is illegal and may be disregarded.

A member of a governmental body may refrain from voting. However, the members of such bodies are under a strong obligation to vote on all motions, because decision-making is one of the primary discretionary duties of the office to which they were elected or appointed. A public officer should refrain from voting only when there is a conflict between personal interest and the interest of the body. The circumstances in which there are conflicts of interest are defined in detail by the statutes of most states.

A member of a governmental body cannot vote on a measure in which the member has a direct personal or financial interest, except in a situation where all other members have the same direct personal or financial interest. For example, a member of a commission could not vote on a motion to fix the sum of money allotted for expenses if he or she were the only member planning to attend a convention, but if all the other members planned to attend the convention and were joined in the motion to fix the sum allotted for expenses, all of them could vote on the motion. If this were not true, in many instances governmental bodies could not act on matters involving public interest. A member of a governmental body cannot vote by proxy or by absentee ballot.

When a governmental body is required to vote on a question, the body cannot delegate this duty to anyone else nor can it direct the secretary to cast a ballot for a particular candidate or measure.

Vacancies

Vacancies in appointive bodies are filled by the original appointing power. Elective bodies sometimes have the right by law to fill vacancies until the next election, at which time the voters elect a person to fill the office. In some instances a special election is called.

Removal of Members

Congress and state legislatures are granted by their constitutions the power to judge the election and qualifications of their members and to remove them under certain conditions and procedures. Governmental boards, councils, commissions, and committees do not have this authority, however, nor have they inherent power to discipline or remove their own members. Statutory law provides procedures by which both appointed and elected members of governmental bodies can be removed for valid cause. Grounds for such removal are usually gross neglect of duty, incompetence, dishonesty, or conviction of a felony or other serious crime.

Appointive members of these public bodies, who hold office at the pleasure of the appointing power, can usually be removed at any time by the appointing power.

Elected members of governmental boards, councils, commissions, and committees can usually be removed only by those who elected them. States that have the recall procedure usually make its provisions applicable to elected members of these bodies.

Parliamentary Authority

Governmental bodies have the right and duty to supplement statutory procedures or those of their adopted rules by the adoption of a book on parliamentary law, such as *The Standard Code of Parliamentary Procedure.* This parliamentary authority governs the procedure of the body in all situations not otherwise provided for by law or by the adopted rules of the body.

Rights of Citizens Attending Meetings

Citizens have the right to attend the meetings of most governmental bodies and they may be permitted to address the body on subjects relevant to its business. However, citizens must observe all the rules and regulations of the body regarding attendance and addressing its members.

Members of the public attending the meetings of governmental bodies do not have the right to interrupt or heckle. They have the right only to seek permission to be heard or to ask questions in accordance with whatever provisions for hearing public opinions or answering questions are fixed by law or have been adopted as rules of the body. They also have the right to submit written petitions, protests, and requests for hearings.

Appendix B

SUGGESTED BYLAW PROVISIONS
FOR A LOCAL ORGANIZATION

ARTICLE I. Name

ARTICLE II. Purposes
(If the purposes are stated in a charter, they need not be repeated in the bylaws.)

ARTICLE III. Membership
   A. Classes of membership with eligibility requirements, rights, and privileges of each class (active, associate, honorary, etc.)
   B. Requirements of parent organization if group holds a charter from higher organization
   C. Procedure for membership application and certification

ARTICLE IV. Officers
   A. List of officers of organization
   B. Method of selection
   C. Duties of each officer

ARTICLE V. Board of directors
   A. Membership
      1. Ex-officio members (usually the officers of the organization)
      2. Elected members: qualifications
   B. Officers of board
      1. Qualifications
      2. Selection
   C. Duties and responsibilities of board (usually the duty and power to act for the organization between meetings of the organization)
   D. Executive committee of board
      1. Membership
      2. Duties
   E. Meetings of board
   F. Reports of board and executive committee

249

ARTICLE VI. Meetings
A. Annual: notice, business to be conducted, order of business
B. Regular: notice, usual order of business
C. Special: how called, notice

ARTICLE VII. Committees
A. Standing committees: list of standing committees, number of members, selection, duties, powers, meetings, reports
B. Special committees: provisions for selection

ARTICLE VIII. Finances
A. Budget preparation and adoption
B. Dues: How determined, when delinquent
C. Auditor: How selected, type of report
D. Surety bond for officers and employees

ARTICLE IX. Terms of office
A. Length of term of officers and board members
B. Staggering of terms

ARTICLE X. Elections
A. Time and method of nominating
B. Nominating committee: duties and report
C. Time and method of election
D. Vote necessary to elect

ARTICLE XI. Quorum
A. Meetings of organization
B. Meetings of board

ARTICLE XII. Discipline and expulsion of members
A. Grounds for action
B. Investigation, hearing, final decision
C. Reinstatement

ARTICLE XIII. Parliamentary authority
A. Provision for adoption
B. Scope of application

ARTICLE XIV. Policies
A. Provisions for adoption
B. Vote required for adoption and amendment

ARTICLE XV. Amendments to bylaws
A. Notice, form
B. Method of consideration, vote required

Appendix C

MODEL MINUTES

THE LOUISVILLE DENTAL SOCIETY, INC.

Call to Order

The regular meeting of the Louisville Dental Society, Inc., was called to order on Wednesday, September 12, 1988, at 7:30 P.M. in the auditorium of the Medical Arts Building by President A. B. Coxwell. A quorum was present.

Minutes
Correction

Approval

The minutes of the August 12th meeting were read by the Secretary, John Atkinson. Frank Jordan called attention to an error in omitting the name of James Skaggs from the Dento-Legal Committee. The correction was made, and the minutes were approved as corrected.

Reports
President

President Coxwell reported that a two-day Leadership Institute was planned for January 16–18, to be held at the Audubon Country Club. He asked all members to reserve the date. *Good Committee Techniques* is the subject.

Treasurer

J. L. Walker, Sr., Treasurer, gave the following summary of collections and expenditures from July 1, 1987, to June 30, 1988:

Treasurer's Report

Receipts, 1987–88		
A.D.A., K.D.A., and Local		
Dues 400 @ $100		$40,000
Bank Budget Plan		1,500
	TOTAL	$41,500
Balance on Hand,		
June 1, 1987		3,500
		$45,000
Disbursements		
A.D.A., K.D.A		
400 @ $80		$32,000
National Children's Dental		
Health Week		2,000
Brown Hotel		100
Clinicians' Expense		4,000
	TOTAL	$38,100
Receipts on Hand		$45,000
Disbursed		38,100
Balance on Hand,		
July 1, 1988		$ 6,900

Clinic Committee

A. P. Williams, Chairman of the Clinic Committee, reported on the Summer Clinic held at the University of Louisville.

Program Committee

Ed Buechel, Chairman of the Program Committee, reported that a program listing the meetings and events of the coming year was being printed and would be mailed to each member on January 1.

Unfinished Business

The President called attention to the fact that a motion to contribute $1,500 to the Cleft Palate Clinic of the Kentucky Dental Association, Inc., which was being discussed at the last meeting and which was interrupted by adjournment, should be acted upon.

MOTION
*Donation to Cleft
Palate Clinic*

The motion is "That $1,500 be donated to the Cleft Palate Clinic of the Kentucky Dental Association, Inc." Motion carried.

New Business

MOTION
Permitting Advertisers

It was moved by Burke Coomer "that the editor of the Bulletin be permitted to secure advertisers to help meet the cost of publication."

AMENDMENT

It was moved by Arnold Kirk "that the motion be amended by adding the words 'and that a committee of five be appointed to assist the editor.'" Amendment carried. Motion carried.

INFORMAL DISCUSSION
New Office

It was moved by Bob Thomas "that the question of securing a new office for the society be discussed informally." Motion carried.

MOTION
Lease

The discussion continued for an hour and was terminated by a motion presented by John Atkinson, "that the secretary be directed to sign a lease for six connecting rooms in the Starks Building." Motion carried.

MOTION TO ADJOURN

Moved by Harry Ritter, "that the meeting adjourn." Motion carried.

Adjournment

The meeting adjourned at 10:08 P.M. John Atkinson, *Secretary*

CORRECTION

The word "approved," which was omitted before the word "advertisers" in the motion permitting advertising in the Bulletin, was added. J.A.

APPROVED
as corrected
Oct. 13, 1988

October 10, John Atkinson, *Secretary*

NOTES

Introduction

1   Robert, Sarah Corbin, et al, *Robert's Rules of Order Newly Revised*, Scott, Foresman and Company, Glenville, Illinois, 1981, pp. t8–t31, 265–284.

CHAPTER 1
The Significance of Parliamentary Law

1   Douglas, William O., "Procedural Safeguards in the Bill of Rights," *Journal of the American Judicature Society,* vol. 31 (6): 166–70 (Apr. 1948).

2   McNabb v. U.S. (1943) 318 U.S. 332, 347.

3   Cannon, Clarence, "Rules of Order," *Encyclopaedia Britannica,* Vol. 19, 1964, 632B–634.

CHAPTER 7
Main Motions

1   Cushing, Luther L., *Lex Parliamenteria Americana: Elements of the Law and Practice of Legislative Assemblies in the United States of America,* Sec. 1266, Little, Brown & Company, Boston, 1856.

2   Oleck, Howard L., *Parliamentary Law for Nonprofit Organizations,* American Law Institute–American Bar Association Committee on Continuing Professional Education, Philadelphia, 1979, p. 75 (note 39).

3   Demeter, George, *Demeter's Manual of Parliamentary Law and Procedure,* Little, Brown & Company, Boston, 1969, p. 153: "The rules that 'only one who voted with the prevailing side can move reconsideration' and that 'the same question cannot be reconsidered more than once' are binding only in organizations whose bylaws so prescribe, or whose parliamentary authority so specifies (as do Robert, Demeter, and some others)."

CHAPTER 8
Subsidiary Motions

1   The two-thirds vote requirement for the motion to lay on the table was first suggested by General Henry M. Robert, who wrote (in *Robert's Rules of Order Revised,* p. 109): "The fundamental principles of parliamentary law require a two-thirds vote for every motion that suppresses a main question for the session without free debate. The motion to lay on the table being undebatable, and requiring only a majority vote, and having the highest rank of all subsidiary motions, is in direct conflict with these principles, if used to suppress a question. If habitually used in this way, it should, like the other motions to suppress without debate, require a two-thirds vote."

Chapter 13
Quorum

1   For incorporated associations, statutory law in some states provides lower quorum requirements than a majority in cases where the organization's bylaws are silent on this point. A number of states have adopted a recommendation of the Committee on Corporate Laws of the American Bar Association that in the absence of a bylaw provision, "members holding one-tenth of the votes entitled to be cast on the matter to be voted upon represented in person or by proxy shall constitute a quorum." American Law Institute–American Bar Association Committee on Continuing Professional Education, *Model Nonprofit Corporation Act*, Philadelphia, 1964, p. 11.

Chapter 19
Officers

1   Frankfurter, Felix, *Of Law and Men*, Harcourt, Brace and World, Inc., New York, 1956, p. 119.

Chapter 30
Often-Asked Questions

1   Hills, George S., *Managing Corporate Meetings*, Ronald Press Co., New York, 1977, p. 328.

2   Commonwealth ex rel. *Fox v. Chace*, 403 Pa. 117, 168 A. 2d 569 (1961).

3   *Mann v. City of LeMars*, 109 Iowa 251, 80 N.W. 327, 328 (1899).

4   *In re Brophy*, 13 N.J. Misc. 462, 179 A. 128, 129 (1935). See also *Hanks v. Borelli*, 2 Ariz. App. 589, 411 P. 2d 27 (1966). Some states permit nonprofit corporations to authorize cumulative voting for directors, and some prohibit it. Before making such a bylaw provision, an incorporated association should obtain legal advice regarding applicable state laws.

5   *Parliamentary Journal*, vol. XXV (2): 78 (Apr. 1984).

6   Demeter, George, *Demeter's Manual of Parliamentary Law and Procedure*, Little, Brown and Co., Boston, 1969, p. 6.

7   Robert, Sarah Corbin, et al, *Robert's Rules of Order Newly Revised*, Scott, Foresman and Company, Glenville, Illinois, 1981, p. 283.

DEFINITIONS OF PARLIAMENTARY TERMS

Adhere   To be attached to and dependent on; pending amendments *adhere* to the motion to which they are applied.

Ad hoc Committee   See *Special Committee.*

Adjourn   To officially terminate a meeting.

Adjourned Meeting   See *Continued Meeting.*

Adjournment Sine Die (without day)   The final adjournment terminating a convention or series of meetings.

Adopt   To approve by vote and give effect to a motion or a report.

Affirmative Vote   The "yes" or "aye" vote supporting a motion as stated.

Agenda   The official list of items of business planned for consideration during a meeting or convention.

Apply   A motion is said to *apply* to another motion when it may be used to alter, dispose of, or affect the first motion.

Approval of Minutes   Formal acceptance, by vote of the members or by general consent, of the secretary's record of a meeting, thus making the record the official minutes of the organization.

Assembly   A meeting of the members of a deliberative body.

Ballot Vote   The expression by ballot, voting machine, or otherwise, of a choice with respect to any election or vote taken on any matter, cast in such a manner that the person expressing the choice cannot be identified with the choice expressed; i.e., a secret ballot.

Bylaws   The set of rules adopted by an organization defining its structure and governing its functions.

Call of a Meeting   The written announcement distributed to members prior to the meeting indicating the time and place of the meeting, and stating the business that is to be brought up at the meeting.

Chair   The presiding officer of a deliberative body.

Challenging a Vote   Objecting to a vote on the ground that the voter does not have the right to vote.

Challenging an Election   Objecting to an election on the ground that it is not being conducted properly.

Charter   An official grant from government of the right to operate as an incorporated organization, or an official grant from a parent organization of the right to operate as a constituent or component group of the parent organization.

Close Debate   A motion which, if passed, ends discussion and prevents further amendments. The old terminology for this motion is "move the previous question." The term "vote immediately" also is sometimes used.

Common Parliamentary Law   The body of rules and principles that is applied by the courts in deciding litigation involving the procedure of organizations. It does not include statutory law or particular rules adopted by an organization.

Consent Agenda   A section of an organization's agenda including only routine matters which are expected to be approved without discussion and without dissent. Any member desiring to discuss or oppose an item can remove it from the consent agenda. Also known as a *consent calendar* or a *unanimous consent agenda.*

Constituent or Component Groups   Subordinate groups making up a parent state, national, or international organization and chartered by it.

Continued Meeting   A meeting that is a resumption at a later specified time of an earlier regular or special meeting. The continued meeting is legally a part of the original meeting. Sometimes called an *adjourned* meeting.

Convene   To open a meeting or convention, usually a large and formal one.

Cumulative Voting   The casting of more than one vote for a candidate when several offices are to be filled, instead of voting for as many candidates as there are vacancies.

Debate   Formal discussion of a motion or proposal by members under the rules of parliamentary law.

Delegation of Authority   An assignment by one person or group to another person or group of the authority to act for the first person or group in certain matters that are lawful and capable of being delegated.

Demand   An assertion of a parliamentary right by a member.

Dilatory Tactics   Misuse of procedures or debate to delay or prevent progress in a meeting.

Discretionary Duty   A duty that usually cannot be delegated to another because members rely on the special intelligence, skill, or ability of the person chosen to perform the duty.

Disposition of a Motion   Action on a motion by voting on it, referring, postponing, or in some way removing it from the consideration of the assembly.

Division of the Assembly   A standing vote.

Division of the Question   Separation of a motion into two or more parts to be discussed and voted upon independently.

En bloc   As a group.

Ex officio Member   One who is a member of a committee or board by reason of holding another office; a treasurer is often an *ex officio member* of the finance committee.

Executive Session   Any meeting of a committee or organization which only members may attend unless others are requested by the body to attend.

Floor (as in *have the floor*)   When a member receives formal recognition from the presiding officer, that member *has the floor* and is the only member entitled to make a motion or to speak.

General Consent   An informal method of approving routine motions by assuming unanimous approval unless objection is raised. Also called *unanimous consent*.

Germane Amendment   An amendment relating directly to the subject of the motion to which it is applied.

Hearing   A meeting of an authorized group for the purpose of listening to the views of members or others on a particular subject.

Hostile Amendment   An amendment that is opposed to the spirit or purpose of the motion to which it is applied.

Illegal Ballot   A ballot that cannot be counted because it does not conform to the rules governing ballot voting.

Immediately Pending Question   The last-proposed of several pending motions and therefore open for immediate consideration.

Incidental Motion   One of a class of motions dealing not with the content of the pending motion but with a procedural question arising incidentally from its consideration. Examples are point of order, parliamentary inquiry, suspension of the rules, division of the question, appeal from the ruling of the chair. Incidental motions have no order of precedence.

Incorporate   To form a group into a legal entity chartered by government and recognized by law as having special rights, duties, and liabilities distinct from those of its members.

Informal Consideration   Consideration and discussion of a problem or motion without the usual restrictions on debate.

Inherent Right   A right or power that is possessed without being derived from another source.

In Order   Permissible and correct from a parliamentary standpoint at a particular time.

Lay on the Table   See *Table*.

Main Motion   A motion which brings business before the assembly.

Majority   A number that is more than half of any given total.

Majority Rule   Rule by decision of the majority of those who actually vote, regardless of whether a majority of those entitled to vote do so.

Majority Vote   More than half of the number of legal votes cast for a particular motion or candidate, unless a different basis for determining the majority is required.

Mass Meeting   See *Organizing Meeting.*

Meeting   An official assembly of the members of an organization during which there is no separation of the members except for a recess, and which continues until adjournment.

Member in Good Standing   Any person who has fulfilled the requirements for membership in the particular organization and who has neither voluntarily resigned nor been suspended or expelled from membership.

Minority   Any number that is less than half of any given total.

Minutes   The legal record of the actions of a deliberative body that has been approved by vote of the body.

Motion   A proposal submitted to an assembly for its consideration and decision; it is introduced by the words, "I move...."

Multiple Slate   A list of offices and candidates containing the names of more than one nominee for an office or offices.

Nomination   The formal proposal to an assembly of a person as a candidate for an office.

Nonprofit Corporation   A corporation whose basic and dominant purposes are ethical, moral, or social, and which distributes no profit to its members.

Objection   The formal expression of opposition to a proposed action.

Order of Business   The adopted order in which the various classifications of business are presented to the meetings of an assembly.

Organizing Meeting   The initial meeting of a group which does not have an established membership roster or rules, sometimes called a *mass meeting.*

Out of Order   Not correct, from a parliamentary standpoint, at the particular time.

Parliamentary Authority   The code or rulebook specified in an organization's bylaws as its authority in matters not covered by its bylaws or standing rules.

Pending Question   Any motion that has been proposed and stated to the assembly for consideration and that is awaiting decision by vote.

Plurality Vote   A larger vote than that received by any opposing candidate or alternative measure.

Point of Order   The raising of a question as to the propriety of some action taken by the chair or by a member.

Policy   An adopted statement of a belief, philosophy, or practice of an organization.

Precedence   The rank or priority governing the proposal, consideration, and disposal of motions.

Precedent   A course of action that may serve as a guide or rule for future similar situations in the particular organization.

Preferential Ballot   A ballot on which the voter indicates more than one choice, and the order of preference, so that second and subsequent choices can be taken into consideration without another election being needed because of failure of any candidate (or proposition) to obtain a majority on the first ballot.

Previous Notice   The announcement in advance, either at the preceding meeting or in the call of the meeting, that a particular subject will be considered at a meeting.

Previous Question   See *Close Debate.*

Privileged Motion   A motion not related to the pending business, but of such urgency that it should be allowed to interrupt pending business, to be decided generally without discussion. Privileged motions include questions of privilege and the motions to recess and to adjourn.

Procedural Motion   A motion that presents a question of procedure as distinguished from a substantive proposition.

Proposal or Proposition   A statement of a motion of any kind for consideration and action.

Proxy   A signed statement authorizing a person to cast the vote of the person signing it. Proxy may also refer to the person who casts the vote.

Putting the Question   The statement, by the presiding officer, of a motion to the assembly for the purpose of taking the vote on it.

Qualified Motion   A motion that is limited or modified in some way in its effect by additional words or provisions, for example, "I move we adjourn *at four o'clock.*"

Question   Any proposal submitted to an assembly for decision.

Quorum   The number or proportion of members that must be present at a meeting of an organization to enable it to act legally on business.

Railroading   To push a motion through so rapidly that members do not have opportunity to exercise their parliamentary rights.

Recess   A brief interruption of a meeting.

Recognition   Formal acknowledgment by the presiding officer of a particular member, giving that member the sole right to speak or to present a motion.

Renew a Motion   To present again a motion previously lost at the same meeting or convention.

Request   A statement to the presiding officer of some right that a member desires to exercise. A request can amount to a demand; for example, a call for division.

Rescind   To repeal a motion which has been passed.

Resolution   A formal motion, usually in writing, and introduced by the word "Resolved," that is presented to an assembly for decision.

Restricted Debate   Debate on certain motions in which discussion is restricted to a few specified points.

Ruling   Any pronouncement of the presiding officer that relates to the procedure of the assembly.

Second   After a motion has been proposed, the statement "I second the motion" by another member who thus indicates willingness to have the motion considered.

Seriatim   Consideration by sections or paragraphs.

Single Slate   A list of offices and candidates containing the name of only one candidate for each office.

Special Committee   A committee that is selected to carry out a particular task, and that ceases to exist once the task is completed. Also called an ad hoc committee.

Special Meeting   A meeting held at a time other than that at which the organization normally meets, called to handle one or more specific matters, which must be noted in the call to the meeting.

Specific Main Motion   A main motion that is so frequently used that it has acquired a specific name to distinguish it from the general main motion; for example, the motion to rescind.

Standing Committee   A committee that has a fixed term of office and that performs any work in its field assigned to it by the bylaws or referred to it by the organization, the board, or the presiding officer.

Statute   A law passed by a legislative body, as a *statute* of Congress.

Statutory Law   Law that is enacted by legislative bodies.

Subsidiary Motion   A motion which changes the main motion or disposes of it or aids in consideration of either a main motion or another motion. Subsidiary motions include to amend, to refer to committee, to postpone definitely, to limit or extend debate, to close debate, and to postpone temporarily.

Substantive Motion   A motion that states a concrete proposal of business as opposed to a procedural matter.

Substitute Motion   The form of amendment that offers a new motion on the same subject, as an alternative to the original motion.

Suspension of the Rules   A vote to disregard temporarily a rule that prevents the assembly from taking a particular action.

Table   To set a motion aside until the assembly decides to resume consideration of it.

Teller   A member appointed to help conduct an election and help count the votes.

Term of Office   The duration of service for which a member is elected or appointed to an office.

Tie Vote   A vote in which the affirmative and negative votes are equal on a motion, or a vote in an election in which two or more candidates receive the same number of votes. A motion receiving a tie vote is lost, since a majority vote is required to take an action. Candidates receiving a tie vote may be voted on until one is elected or the assembly votes to break the tie in some other way.

Unanimous Consent   See *General Consent.*

Unanimous Vote   A vote without any dissenting vote. One adverse vote prevents a unanimous vote.

Unfinished Business   Any business that is postponed definitely to the next meeting or that was pending and interrupted by adjournment of the previous meeting.

Voice Vote   A vote taken by calling for "ayes" and "noes" and judged by volume of voice response; sometimes called a *viva voce* vote.

Vote Immediately   An alternate term for the motion to close debate.

Waiver of Notice   Act of relinquishing the right to have had notice of a proposal or meeting. Also may refer to the statement proving the relinquishment of notice.

Write-in Vote   A vote for someone who has not been nominated, cast by writing in on the ballot the name of the person.

Order of precedence	Can interrupt?	Requires second?	Debatable?	Amendable?
PRIVILEGED MOTIONS				
1. Adjourn	No	Yes	No	No
2. Recess	No	Yes	Yes†	Yes†
3. Question of privilege	Yes	No	No	No
SUBSIDIARY MOTIONS				
4. Postpone temporarily (Table)	No	Yes	No	No
5. Close debate	No	Yes	No	No
6. Limit debate	No	Yes	Yes†	Yes†
7. Postpone definitely	No	Yes	Yes†	Yes†
8. Refer to committee	No	Yes	Yes†	Yes†
9. Amend	No	Yes	Yes	Yes
MAIN MOTIONS				
10. a. The main motion	No	Yes	Yes	Yes
b. Specific main motions				
Reconsider	Yes	Yes	Yes†	No
Rescind	No	Yes	Yes	No
Resume consideration	No	Yes	No	No

INCIDENTAL

No order of precedence	Can interrupt?	Requires second?	Debatable?	Amendable?
MOTIONS				
Appeal	Yes	Yes	Yes	No
Suspend rules	No	Yes	No	No
Consider informally	No	Yes	No	No
REQUESTS				
Point of order	Yes	No	No	No
Parliamentary inquiry	Yes	No	No	No
Withdraw a motion	Yes	No	No	No
Division of question	No	No	No	No
Division of assembly	Yes	No	No	No

*Requires two-thirds vote when it would suppress a motion without debate.
†Restricted.

GOVERNING MOTIONS

Vote required?	Applies to what other motions?	Can have what other motions applied to it?	Refer to page
Majority	None	None	72
Majority	None	Amend†	70
None	None	None	66
Majority*	Main motion	None	62
2/3	Debatable motions	None	58
2/3	Debatable motions	Amend†	56
Majority	Main motion	Amend†, close debate, limit debate	53
Majority	Main motion	Amend†, close debate, limit debate	50
Majority	Rewordable motions	Close debate, limit debate	42
Majority	None	Specific main, subsidiary	30
Majority	Main motion	Close debate, limit debate	33
Majority	Main motion	Close debate, limit debate	37
Majority	Main motion	None	39

MOTIONS

Vote required?	Applies to what other motions?	Can have what other motions applied to it?	Refer to page
Majority	Decision of chair	Close debate, limit debate	77
2/3	None	None	79
Majority	Main motion	None	120
None	Any error	None	83
None	All motions	None	86
None	All motions	None	89
None	Main motion	None	91
None	Indecisive vote	None	94

THE CHIEF PURPOSES OF MOTIONS

PURPOSE	MOTION
Present an idea for consideration and action	Main motion Resolution Consider informally
Improve a pending motion	Amend Division of question
Regulate or cut off debate	Limit or extend debate Close debate
Delay a decision	Refer to committee Postpone definitely Postpone temporarily Recess
Suppress a proposal	Table Withdraw a motion
Meet an emergency	Question of privilege Suspend rules
Gain information on a pending motion	Parliamentary inquiry Request for information Request to ask member a question Question of privilege
Question the decision of the presiding officer	Point of order Appeal from decision of chair
Enforce rights and privileges	Division of assembly Division of question Parliamentary inquiry Point of order Appeal from decision of chair
Consider a question again	Resume consideration Reconsider Rescind Renew a motion
Change an action already taken	Reconsider Rescind Amend by new motion
Terminate a meeting	Adjourn Recess

INDEX

ACKNOWLEDGMENTS

The revision committee is indebted to many individuals and organizations for suggestions and assistance in the preparation of this edition of the *Standard Code*. Officers and members of the American Medical Association and the American Dental Association and their affiliated organizations have been especially forthcoming in sharing their views, as have members of the Commission on American Parliamentary Practice.

Individuals who have provided counsel and advice include Leo Athans, Lee Demeter, H. W. Farwell, Thomas J. Gmeinder, Robert W. Leiman, J. David Lofton, C. Barry McCarty, Emil Pfister, Gregg Phifer, Virginia Schlotzhauer, Kim Stuart, William Tacey, and Leona White. Special appreciation is expressed to Floyd M. Riddick, parliamentarian emeritus of the United States Senate, for his assistance.

The listing of these organizations and individuals should not be construed as an endorsement by them of all of the changes that were made in the *Standard Code*. It was often necessary to balance differing viewpoints and weigh them against established customs and precedents. The revision committee accepts full responsibility for decisions made in such cases.